SAAB 99 AND 900

The Complete Story

SAAB 99 AND 900
The Complete Story

Lance Cole

First published in 2001 by
The Crowood Press Ltd
Ramsbury, Marlborough
Wiltshire SN8 2HR

British Library Cataloguing-in-Publication Data
A catalogue record for this book is available from
the British Library.

ISBN 1 86126 429 1

Dedication
For my daughter, Emily

Acknowledgements
This book would not have happened without the help of many
people who have given generously of their time, including car
designer Bjorn Envall, Chris and Shelagh Day, Colin Wallace,
Richard Elliot, William Glander, and others in the Saab Owners
Club, and enthusiasts' groups. Thanks are also due to the Gunnel
Ekburg and Gunvor Thorson in the Saab press office at Trollhattan,
to Per-Borje Elg and Peter Backstrom at Saab, and to other
enthusiasts at Saab UK, Newbury/Reading Saab, Red Post
Garage Newton Abbot and Just Saab Garage.

Photos are from the Saab Archive and the author.

Designed and typeset by
Focus Publishing, 11a St Botolph's Road,
Sevenoaks, Kent TN13 3AJ

Printed and bound in Great Britain by The Bath Press

Contents

The face of Saab – the Classic 900 saloon with the slant nose of 1988.

The Turbo badge and the legendary 'Inca' wheels.

6

Introduction

SVENSK BIL MED FLYGKVALITET – SWEDISH CAR WITH AIRCRAFT QUALITY

Svenska Aeroplan Aktiebolaget, or Saab, is distinguished among the mainstream European car makers of the 1970s, 80s and 90s as a manufacturer that dared to be different. This aircraft company's cars ignored the contradictions of perceived wisdom in motor manufacture, capturing the spirit of those who designed and built them.

What is that certain 'Saabness'? According to Saab enthusiast and car designer Jim Das, the designs of the 'broad-shouldered Swedes', the 99 and 900, 'have a timeless appeal that does not date because they were not a response to a fashion trend, as most car design is' (Royal College of Art auto design degree presentation, featuring a future vision for Saab). Legendary rally driver Eric Carlsson described the purchase of a Saab as a 'long-term choice [rather than] a fashion statement'. Saab's cars always appealed to a certain kind of car buyer – someone who appreciated the excellent engineering, the advanced safety features and aerodynamics, and the unusual character of the design.

It was the 99 and 900, especially the turbo models, that put Saab on the map. Daring to be different and yet remaining committed to practicality, strength, safety and reliability, and quality, the Saab company created a unique character. Its personality has endured for more than half a century and today, despite ownership by General Motors, it remains individual. The 900 MkI – the Classic 900 – and the 99, are fine examples of that individualism. They remain icons in the history of the motor car; indeed, the last-of-the-line 900s attained instant classic car status and are now highly sought after.

Saab 99 & 900: The Complete Story traces the development from the early days of the 99 prototype (or Project Gudmund) to the 900 Turbo 16 'Ruby', which signalled the end of the pure Saab, and the beginning of the next 900 under Saab's new parent General Motors. It tells the story of the men who were the driving force behind Saab – design genius Sixten Sason, Gunnar Ljungstrom and Rolf Mellde, and others, who created the first Saab car in 1947; Stan Wennlo, who promoted the later turbo cars; and Bjorn Envall, the designer of the 900. It focuses on the safety and the aerodynamics, the engines and the handling of the 900 – all the Saab hallmarks that made the car a worldwide classic – and its survival through to production.

At one time, the Saab car was seen simply as a workhorse for the Swedish people. From these humble beginnings, within a few years, the British and the Americans were seeing Saabs as upmarket cars of a certain class. The Swedish Royal family – from King Gustaf Adolf VI and King Carl Gustaf XVI to Prince Bertil – became Saabists through and through.

Saabs may have gone from workhorses to luxury cars, but the essential qualities of the originals were never forgotten. Volvo may have benefited from a certain 'Scandinavian' identity later on in its history, but its original designs were hardly innovative. All those years ago, it was Saab that came up with a car that was unique, advanced and daring – yet was still a car

Saab 99 & 900 Evolution

Note: Saab models for next model year were announced in the last week of August or the first week of September the preceding year. Revised model production began late in same year (November/December), with new model year cars arriving in showrooms after Christmas.

22 November 1967:	99 unveiled to the press
29 November 1967:	British press previews the 99
1967–68:	99's year-long development programme; cars placed with evaluation customers
1968:	99 two-door launched on to LHD European market
April 1969:	American 99 sales launched
1 November 1969:	RHD British cars on sale
13 April 1970:	new four-door body style for 99 launched (the first four-door Saab). New Finnish factory builds some 99s. Spec of early 99s improved. Automatic 99 EA launched in Sweden and Europe then UK with fuel injection; American cars get manual box with fuel injection
1971:	revised dashboard and instrument panel design; larger 1854cc engine
1972:	'rubber bumper' cars – styling revisions to 99 chrome grille and bumpers changed; headlamp wipers; side-impact doorbars added
1973:	1.7-litre engine phased out. 2-litre Swedish-built revised engine offered in 99 EMS sports model, with electronic rather than mechanical injection. Base model X7 99 launched with unique bumpers and trim
1 January 1974:	three-door Combi Coupe 99 launched; 'Wagon Back' in USA
1975:	Belgian production plant starts building 99s
March 1976:	five-door body shell launched
Spring 1976:	luxury GLE 99 models launched
Spring 1977:	EMS-Turbo pre-production cars
December 1977:	Turbo models of 1978 model year cars launched. All 99s receive styling changes – revised lamps/indicator units and trim upgrades. Assembly in Arlov and Uusikaupunki, Finland. Technical spec revisions. Turbo model achieves worldwide fame and sales. Three- then two-door Turbos. Five-door Turbos made for UK market in very small numbers (fewer than 50 cars)
May 1978:	900 launched; sales begin at end of 1978 for 1979 model year. 900 based on 99 but with new front end, major revisions to drivetrain,

suspension, fittings and trim, and entirely new interior. Three- and five-door shells

1979:	900 model debuts on European and American LHD markets; 99 range slimmed down. Trim items added to 900. Most UK 99s have 2-litre engine. Extra 99s produced for UK due to a delay to RHD 900s. Limited edition two-door 99 Turbos in Acacia Green sold in mainland Europe only
1980:	99 continues; 900 gets new seats
1981:	special 99 with direct-injection 118hp engine and luxury trim for Nordic area only. Kerosene-powered special 99 for Finnish market. 900 gets new seats and a new four-door saloon body option
Summer 1982:	all 99s get revised H-series engine. Economy special model 99s for Nordic market; narrow-profile tyres, five-speed box. APC system fitted to 900s
Summer 1983:	revised 99 with 900 trim additions and centre console. 900 two-tone cars debut. 900 EMS trim tag ends, replaced by GLi
1984:	final 99 model year. Finnish-built cars only; many sold in UK
15 March 1985:	last UK delivery of 99. 900 Turbo 16s – 'Aero' – in mainland Europe and latterly in the UK after T16s badge tag
Summer 1985:	revised 99 launched as Saab 90 – 99 two-door with new 900 two-door rear end replacing original 99 rear body. Trim and spec upgrades. Revisions to 900. Saab-Scania badging
1986:	minor changes to 90. 900 16-valve engines expanded in range
1987:	90 model withdrawn. 900 gets new sloping nose styling. 900 convertible on sale worldwide
1988:	engineering changes to turbo units in 900s
1989:	900 8-valve ends production. 900 range revised
1990:	all 900s are made with 16 valves
1991:	uprated 2119cc engine introduced on certain markets
1992:	anti-lock brakes on all 900s
1993:	final 900s, 'Ruby' model, with special trim, uprated bhp. No body kit
26 March 1993:	900 production ends after 15 years, with 908,817 cars produced

	Saab Innovations
1947:	Saab's first car, the 92 model, a front-drive, aerodynamically tuned, flat-floored car launched with reinforced body shell built on aeronautical design theories. Transverse engine of two-stroke design. Independent suspension
1953:	factory-fitted front seatbelts
1960:	airflow-tuned cabin ventilation and extraction system
1961:	first use of rear window aerofoil 'slicer' to clean vertical rear windscreen on an estate car body
1963:	diagonal spilt braking system
1967:	Saab 99 with advanced safety-cage body, tuned aerodynamics, crushable steering column, starter switch between seats for safety reasons (removes key from leg impact area on fascia); front-driven via 15in wheels
1969:	headrests of proper safety design, rather than just for comfort
1971:	self-repairing cell-construction 5mph rubber bumpers; headlamp wipers and washers as standard; heated front seats
1972:	proper side-impact protection via box-section steel support beam linked to lateral compression panels; impact-absorbing roof linings
1976:	USA-spec cars get catalysts
1977:	birth of the Saab Turbo – mass-market application of unique Saab-designed waste-gate turbocharger design in 99 model. 900 model launched – notable for unique cabin air filter system and safety body design, and turbocharging refinements. Automatic Performance Control: Saab-designed APC system to fine-tune engine under its own self-management system
1982:	asbestos-free brake pads on all Saabs
1983:	16-valve 2-litre engine with unusual cylinder head design to promote combustion and fuel efficiency
1985:	direct ignition system; automatic seatbelt tensioners
1986:	Saab 9000 becomes the first front-driven car in the world to have ABS
1990:	900 cars get the pioneering Saab light-pressure turbo unit
1991:	Saab launches first CFC-free air-conditioning system
1993:	first clutchless manual/auto gearbox via Saab 'Sensonic' design. Night vision dashboard display
1996:	active headrest – safety-enhancing head restraint adaptive system
1997:	ventilated front seats with in-built fan

for the masses. The 92 was a real feat of engineering and advanced design, yet it did not achieve the same sort of publicity as, for example, the Mini. At the time of the 92, Issigonis was still turning out leaf-sprung, rear-driven cars, such as the Morris Minor 1000. Europe's car makers were following all sorts of different design routes. British company Alvis of Coventry had experimented with front-wheel drive, with a front-driven grand prix racer in 1926 and a road-going version of the same, with all-round independent suspension, in 1928; Cord, Adler and DKW had also tried front-wheel drive from 1930 to 1935; Citroen may have launched front-wheel drive in the 1934 Traction Avant, but it was Saab that pioneered the front-drive concept for mass use in a medium-sized car. (The 2CV was something else entirely!)

Saab's teardrop-shaped car, with its front drive, transverse engine and monocoque safety body, was a major milestone in the history of car design. Yet the achievement of Sason, Mellde and Ljungstrom did not receive the public recognition it deserved. Perhaps it was because they were unassuming Swedes, rather than fashionable Italians.

Tucked away in Scandinavia, Saab was hardly a household name elsewhere in the world. Yet this small company from a small country did not ignore world markets. The company created the 92 model for its own home market, but the car turned out to be so good that it sold successfully worldwide. A marque was created that led to the creation of the 99 and the 900, the high point of all that was Saab.

Saab reached all corners of the world – in the late 1980s, in Aspen, Colorado, USA, the sheriff, the entire police force, and large numbers of the locals were driving Saab 900s. In Solvang, California, USA, the whole town is built in Swedish style, the high street is packed with Saabs and the local garage deals day in, day out with Saabs old and new. Saabs found their way to Singapore, Malaysia and Indonesia, and there is a dynamic Saab owners' club in Japan. All over Europe, every country has a network of owners' clubs and groups of dedicated Saab fanatics, or 'Saabists'.

In late 1979, the black 99 Turbo, with its 'Inca' wheels, was the car to be seen in in London. In the early 1980s, the stylish black, dark blue or dark green metallic 900 Turbo – classless yet classy – was enormously popular in London, Frankfurt, Amsterdam and Stockholm. It became a thinking person's urban style icon, yet different versions of the 99 and 900 were equally at home in a rural environment. Some Saabs became 'must-have' cars on the eastern seaboard of the USA, while in Tokyo, the 900 became a design icon, a real mark of being different.

The spirit of Saab, the unassuming car maker, is part of its appeal. BMW and Mercedes may be more famous, Volvo may be bigger these days, Citroen may have returned to daring to be different, but Saab will always be unique. The breadth of its cars' design and its engineering achievements remained unheralded for so long. This is the first book dedicated to the modern-day Saabs that were also the last of the old, purists' Saabs – the amazing Saab story is well worth telling.

Lance Cole, Wiltshire

1   Saab – Before the 99

COMPANY ROOTS

Car marketing people today aim to give many brands an allure of history or heritage. In truth, few manufacturers can claim roots as illustrious and relevant as the adverts imply. Saab's lineage, however, stands head and shoulders above the rest. These days, Saab may trade heavily upon its aviation history in its marketing, yet there really is aeronautical design in all of its cars. Saab was (and still is) a maker of aeroplanes; its name, Svenska Aeroplan Aktiebolaget, translates literally as 'Swedish Aeroplane Company Ltd'. In 1957, the firm's car-making arm became simply Saab Aktiebolaget, dispensing with the

'Aeroplan'. Aerodynamics, and structure and function allied to form, are a vital part of the Saab design story.

Saab's roots lay in the industrial town of Trollhättan, where, in the 1920s and 30s, a number of small firms were involved in light and heavy engineering. There was a ready and skilled workforce, and the Gota river was an important hydroelectric resource. Members of a prominent family called Wallenberg recognized the need for a workhorse car that could handle Sweden's weather, and would sell well in the post-war economic environment. Gunnar Philipson, head of the Philipsons Automobil AB garage chain, contributed substantial funds towards Saab's first car project. (In return,

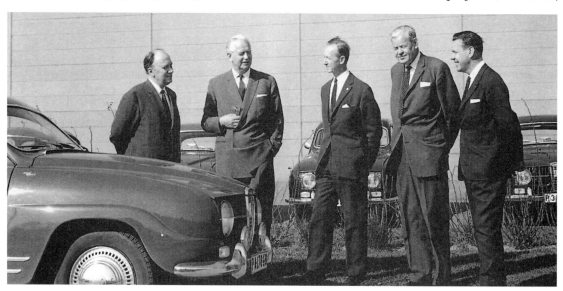

The Saab team: (left to right) Svante Holm, Trggve Holm, Gunnar Ljungstrom, Sixten Sason, Rolf Mellde, the men who directed and designed the first Saab car in 1946.

12

Philipson was granted sales rights, which were later taken back in-house by Saab.)

By the mid-1930s, Sweden was becoming concerned about industrial strength and rearmament. In 1936, a combined aircraft company was created by the Swedish government, with the merger of a number of small aircraft makers. All based near Linköping and Trollhättan, they had mostly been involved in building German, British and French aircraft designs and engines under licence. Aeroplanvarvet I Skane (AVIS, later AETA-AB), set up by Dr Enoch Thulin, dated back to 1914. AETA-AB had become a serious engine and airframe builder, turning out nearly a hundred aircraft, but by the late 1920s, Sweden's aviation business had declined. Among the other companies involved in the combined company were ASJA (Swedish Railway Works), Nohab (Nydqvist and Holm), Svenska Aero (licence-building German airframe parts), and Flygindustri from Malmo, which had links with Junkers. Armament manufacturer Bofors also played a role in expanding the sector between the wars; eventually, Saab Aero was to buy Bofors. But it was AETA that had produced aircraft engines in large numbers up to the 1920s and even designed and built its first Swedish aircraft type at that time. A reserve of aeronautical engineering was well established in this part of Sweden and the new company represented the true beginning of Saab.

During the 1920s and 30s, success for these firms came and went. By 1937, most of the big fish had absorbed the smaller ones; with the threat of war, a government decree created a larger aviation enterprise from the merger of companies owned by Bofors and Nohab. The Swedish Air Force needed to be re-equipped, yet, because of Sweden's uncertain position in Europe, the German, British and American aviation industries were unable to continue their

involvement. The Swedish aviation industry had to start from scratch. In 1937, Gunnar Dellner headed the umbrella company of Svenska Aeroplan Aktiebolaget, under Chairman Torsten Nothin and President Ragnar Wahrgren. The amalgamation in April 1937 also involved engine makers, and the remaining aviation division of railway engineering firm ASJA, of Linköping. The complex set-up was clarified under Axel Wenner-Gren in 1939, with a reorganization of the various groups and their spheres of influence. Saab took control of the ASJA interests, and was itself later sold off to the Wallenbergs.

AERONAUTICAL HERITAGE

Ragnar Wahrgren headed Saab from 1939–50 and was one of the Saab men who approved the first Saab car project. Frid Wanstrom, who headed the Saab research division and was responsible for the advanced aerodynamics that distinguished Saab's early aeroplanes, along with Lars Brising, Eric Bratt, A.J. Andersson, Hans Eric Lofkvist, gave Saab aircraft swept wings, leading-edge slats, double delta profiles and a highly efficient structure. All the new features were checked out by Saab's designers in the company's own wind tunnels. Saab aeroplanes were known for their efficiency of design, their superb handling and aerodynamics and their general 'feel' – just like the cars bred from them.

Sweden's aeronautical industry benefited from the vision of forward-looking men who were eager to turn their engineering skills to modification of successful designs, and to innovation, creating in the process their own motifs. These impressive skills represent a core theme in the history of Saab aeroplane and car manufacture. Much of Saab's aeronautical work is carried out in conjunction with the design of its cars. Geographically

The Saab J29 'Tunnan' – Saab's advanced swept wing jet fighter of the late 1950s, a fine example of Saab's aviation design skills.

isolated, employees at Saab's aircraft design centre at Linköping toiled away, developing advanced aerodynamics and structures, and airframes offering superb handling. It was many years before their genius was recognized worldwide.

The earliest Saab-built aircraft, such as the B3 and B5, were licence-built variants of modified designs from American and German manufacturers. Saab's first aircraft built to its own design, in 1937, was the prop-powered, single-engined Saab 17, followed by the Saab twin-engined bomber (the 18 model). The next move was an intriguing twin-boomed affair with pusher prop – the 21 fighter – which was re-

---

Major revisions 93–96 models

Longitudinal-mounted 748cc three-cylinder engine (1955)
Updated 841cc unit (1960)
V4 1498cc (1967)
Coil springs (1955)
First revised nose styling 1956 (93 model)
Restyled doors and rear end with larger rear windscreen 96 model (1960)
Longer bonnet and new nose (1965)
Interior updates and trim changes

engineered into a jet-powered version named the 21R. After the war came the Saab Scandia airliner, a sort of twin-engined Swedish competitor to the Douglas DC-3. The Scandia was so advanced and so well engineered that many remained in airline service into the 1960s. Two highly successful light trainers – the 91 Safir and the Saab 105 jet trainer – followed in the 1950s, but it was the Saab Lansen, Draken and Tunnan jet air-craft that really made Saab's mark in the aviation world. Their features were advanced; the Draken was notable for its double delta-wing shape and high speed, the Tunnan for its early use of a swept wing, and the Lansen for its handling. In terms of design, they were leading-edge aeroplanes. More recently, the Viggen jet fighter, the 340 model airliner and the Gripen fighter of the late 1980s underlined Saab's reputation as an aircraft builder.

Saab 92 (series production begun December 1949)

Engine:

Type:	two-cylinder, two-stroke, oil/petrol mix lubrication; transverse-mounted
Bore:	3.15in (80mm)
Stroke:	3in (76mm)
Capacity:	764cc
Compression ratio:	6.6/1
Fuel supply:	carburettor
Max power:	25bhp at 3,800rpm

Transmission:
Three-speed gearbox via driveshafts
 Column-mounted shift lever
Manual freewheel economy device

Suspension and Steering:
Independent all round with shock absorbers and rear torsion bar
Rack and pinion steering

Brakes:
Four drums on 15in wheels

Body:
Two-door style unit construction all welded hull
Steel tube and section reinforcements to roof pillars and sill members
Strong centre monocoque hull section
Aerodynamic low drag design
Co-efficient of drag (inc cooling resistance) 0.35 CD

Dimensions:
Track, front and rear 46.5in (1.18m)
Wheelbase 97.2in (2.47m)
Length 154in (3.92m)
Width 64in (1.62m)
Height 56in (1.42m)

Gunnar Ljungstrom: Father of the First Saab Car

In late 1945 – just months after the end of the Second World War – Saab began the process of becoming a car maker. Instructed by the vice-president of Saab's aero division, Sven Otterback, a small department was set up. Twenty draughtsmen and skilled aero engineers were dedicated to creating a prototype. The man appointed to head this new venture was aero engineer and wing stressman Gunnar Ljungstrom.

Bringing his aircraft design and construction skills to Saab's first car, Ljungstrom crafted a car that was efficient, safe and above all technically evolved down to the last millimetre, the last gram, the point of engineering perfection. Given the austere economics of the time, a small team, and only the experiences of others to go on, creating such an individual and advanced car design was surely a remarkable achievement. For example, the transverse engine layout was virtually unheard of at the time. It would have been easier to copy a pre-war design and tweak it a bit, but that would not have

Gunnar Ljungstrom, father of the Saab car.

been Ljungstrom's way. The car was a sensation, setting the tone for the spirit of Saab and going on to breed the 99 and the 900.

Ljungstrom's father, a prolific inventor, had tried to design and build a car in the 1930s – without success. His son had an innate feel for what was needed in the post-war years and, although his ideas were for a Swedish car for the Swedish people, he knew that it would appeal to others in other climes. Ljungstrom crafted the placement of the DKW-derived engine, the chassis and suspension needs of the car – with stress paths and load-bearing members all carefully calculated and placed – but his work needed a body. Saab did not want a flat-fronted, 1930s throwback, but a low-drag shape with a specific look. Ljungstrom called in Sixten Sason.

Ex-pilot Sason was already a well-known industrial designer, his futuristic ideas featuring in many Swedish magazines. By late 1945, he had presented his sketch of the body for the new car – something so different, yet so essentially right, that Ljungstrom and the Saab board knew that it was just what they needed. Bringing in Sason had been an inspired move.

Between them, Ljungstrom and Sason created the look and feel for the first Saab car and then went on to do the same for the 99. Ljungstrom brought aircraft-style body strength and safety to the cars, working out load paths and stress compression routes largely in his head. His structural thinking was greatly advanced; twenty years later, Ford created an aviation-style monocoque with safety section design, using massive resources and an early super computer. Ljungstrom also put a flat bottom undertray in the car in 1947; it took the rest of the motor industry decades to follow suit. And all this happened in a tiny facility, where no car had been built before and resources was limited.

This early pioneer of car safety retired from his position at the head of Saab's engineering department in 1970. He received many honours for his work, notably a fellowship of the Society of Automotive Engineers and a gold medal from the Swedish Academy of Engineering Sciences.

SAAB CAR DESIGN

Many of the men from Saab's aeronautical division also worked for Saab's car division, and cross-fertilization of aviation-inspired ideas frequently took place. Among them were Saab designer Kurt Sjorgen, and Ragnar Haardmark; the man who led the Saab 90 model Scandia airliner project, Tord Lidmalm, later became Technical Director of the Saab-Scania group; A.J. Andersson was Saab aircraft's Chief Designer in the 1940s; Sixten Sason had been an air force pilot in the 1930s, and had worked for Saab's aircraft division from 1941, developing an innate feel for aviation engineering solutions.

In building aircraft, Saab learned the art of stress and load-path management, aerodynamics, dynamic handling, and pilot ergonomics. Much of the knowledge was carried over into the car designs, notably in chassis stress work, safety and cabin/driver controls. Saab had its roots in making fine aeroplanes, many of which achieved worldwide export sales, and knew how to design, engineer and build. It was natural, therefore, that the company should turn its hand to making cars. There was a need and the talent existed to fill that need.

Until that time, Sweden's ready market for cars had been served only by Volvo and by imports, mostly from DKW (part of the giant Auto-Union, Audi-Horch company), Opel and Citroen. The little DKW, particularly, had proved very popular in Sweden, with its two-stroke engine; lubricated with a mix of oil and petrol, it did not suffer in the extremes of cold. The car sold well for Philipsons, but it had a rather pre-war look, with its running boards and wings. There was clearly an opportunity for a modernized, home-grown version. Philipsons' major gamble – helping to finance the first Saab – paid off far more than they could ever have imagined and the Saab 92 turned out to be far more than everyone expected. (Ironically, in later years, DKW produced a small, attractive two-door coupe with overtones of Saab styling.)

Sweden's small population was widely distributed and the Swedish people needed reliable vehicles for long-distance travel. Permafrost, ice and snow created difficult conditions, so a car for Sweden had to be a simple yet strong, fully independent vehicle capable of carrying on with its own problems to the nearest garage. The first Saab car could have been a boxy, easily produced steel 'tractor' with a reliable but agricultural design. The climate did not allow for a curvy, chrome-emblazoned style wagon that was labour-intensive and complicated to build and own. A sort of Swedish Citroen would hardly suit...and yet there was much in Saab's first car that was as revolutionary and curvaceous as some of the Citroens of later years. The new Saab needed a proper chassis to tackle those Swedish roads in the worst conditions.

Swedish car maker Volvo had been making cars since 1927 but, by the 1930s, their designs were heavily based on large American gas-guzzlers. There was no domestically produced, small workhorse car in their range; either Saab or a European competitor would be sure to take up the opportunity. Volvo saw the chance and started to think about a car that was more suited to Sweden's conditions; however, the first 'real' Volvo, the PV444, was a mix-and-match, rear-wheel driven Anglo-American influenced receipe. It was a good car, but it was not immediately identifiable as a car from Sweden, for the Swedish. Engineering innovation was the province of Saab.

Saab's decision to make such a car was timed just right. Their choice of path was a matter of informed risk-taking at a difficult time of post-war socio-economic conservatism.

THE 92 SERIES

The Project

Gunnar Ljungstrom, Rolf Mellde and Sixten Sason are high on the list of credits for Saab's first car (model name 92001). Sven Otterback was one of the Saab directors in the 1940s who pushed for the team to get started on a car project. Tore Svenson was the project engineer. These were the men responsible for the first Saab car and rising among them were Svante Holm and Tryggve Holm, who saw the development of the first 92 into the 93, and beyond.

A planning department was set up in late 1944. By 1945, Sason – already a well-known Swedish designer – had been called in to produce a body to clothe the mechanicals designed by Ljungstrom. Over the next two years, the team worked away on Saab Aeroplan's first car. Mellde was the suspension and handling wizard with a taste for rallying; he gave the car its effective and communicative steering and suspension, and fine front-drive handling and balance. The features all went into the 99 and 900. The result – the Saab 92001 – represented a milestone in car styling and engineering.

In December 1949, the 92 series went into production. In its various incarnations, the series lasted over thirty years and gave Saab the financial capacity to design the 99.

Features

The 92 had front drive and superb aerodynamics (including an undertray, which was unheard of at the time). Its boat-style rear end hinted at Tatra and Hans Ledwinka designs and was similar to Paul Jaray's styling in the 1920s. Later, English aircraft maker Bristol would adopt the Saab rear-end styling for its cars.

The 92's engine design was related to that of the DKW, but was ideal for its purpose and its time. Because of the war, car design had stood still, while engineering and aerodynamics knowledge had moved on. What people needed most was a good solid car that gave no trouble. Trends in car design differed from country to country. Giascosa at Fiat, Porsche at VW, the men at Renault and Ledwinka at Tatra had their minds firmly set on rear-engined cars. Bertoni, Lefebrve and Boulanger at Citroen were out on a limb, designing front-engined, front-driven models. The English were still turning out rear-driven, leaf-sprung cars for their mass market; innovation had yet to become fashionable in this market sector. Some car makers used the old-fashioned chassis with separate body; others tried a combined chassis-monocoque theme.

Saab's move to follow Citroen was quite a gamble, with a small budget and a small team. The Saab 92 was really something different, and the Saab 99 and 900 reinforced that sense of innovation.

With over 50 per cent of its weight over the driven front wheels, and narrow tyres, the 92 romped through snow and ice; Saab's reputation for fine handling was established. The car also had proper rollover protection, with a reinforced roof. At the time, few makers even tested for rollover strength, but the Saab had a high torsional rigidity rating and a strong centre cabin section. The 'steel box sections' of most cars involve pressed-steel formings, welded up to form the hollow pillars of the body monocoque. The Saab had 2.5mm steel rods inserted into double-thickness windscreen pillars and door posts, and the roof pillars could take an extraordinary amount of punishment before failing.

Safety through body strength – a Saab hallmark – was the philosophy and particular skill of Gunnar Ljungstrom, who had previously worked in Saab's aircraft design department. Forces were fed through the structure via fail-safe structures based on classic load-path carrying designs. A central 'tub' was created, with the drive train and

These three shots show the sheer advanced future vision of Sason's styling – the first Saab. In places the car's steel was over 1.5mm thick, giving it great strength.

Sixten Sason: Thinking in Three Dimensions

Born in 1912 in Skovde, Sweden, as Sixten Anderson, Sason adopted the more distinctive surname in order to improve his image in the world of design. The son of a sculptor, Sason studied art in Paris and then trained as a designer. In the 1920s, he learned to fly with the Swedish airforce but was invalided out after an accident, minus one lung.

Bjorn Envall, Sason's successor at Saab design, recalls how he and his extrovert colleague worked well beyond the usual 9 to 5. Often they would try to solve design problems at home or over a drink, and they spent many days touring the motor shows and immersing themselves in new ideas.

In 1946, Sason's first renderings for the 92 – project X9248 – were really advanced. The car had an aerofoil front with a small slotted grille and headlamps hidden under a glass coaming. It was radical, even for the aerodynamics-trained minds at Saab and the production car was slightly modified, with headlamps and a real grille mounted in the front panel.

For the 99, Sason drew on Italian themes and an awareness of American product design to create a distinctive Swedish shape, which, nevertheless, had international appeal. Alongside its contemporaries, the 99 looked fresh and timeless without being gimmicky, and many of its features were found later in other cars.

Sixten Sason, the designer who created the shape that was Saab.

In the 1930s, Sason had become known for his ability not just to style the exterior of a product, but to think about the structure and engineering underneath the styling. He had worked on X-ray, see-through drawings while at Saab Aero. During the war, he is reputed to have sketched the secret inner details of a crashed German rocket, and to have flown them to Intelligence in London in the bomb bay of a Mosquito fighter. His curvaceous, futuristic designs for cars and aircraft were way ahead of their time and after the war, he also designed cameras, most notably the iconic Hasselblad shape, as well as furniture and appliances for major brand names. In the 1960s, Sason made drawings for the 'Katherina', a two-door targa-topped sportster for Saab, from which a running prototype was made. The car never made it into production, but it displayed styling themes that would be seen years later in cars from other makers.

The 92 may have been Sason's most visually stunning automotive sculpture – with its perfection of form, allied to function and efficiency of airflow – but perhaps it is the Saab 99, with its maturity and wholeness of design that became the greatest tribute to his abilities.

Bjorn Envall, Sason's young student, who succeeded him as head of design at Saab in the 1970s and 80s, remembers the designer's wit, style and expansive thinking. Sason was no egotist and was generous in his encouragement of Envall and others. Ljungstrom described him as 'a genius; an engineer with the talents of an artist, or an artist with the temperament of an engineer...the ideal partner to work with'.

Sixten Sason, design artist, engineer, visionary and humourist, struggled for years on one lung, and died in 1967, just before his Saab 99 shape took to the roads.

One of Sixten Sason's early sketches for the 92, dating from around 1946.

extremities being carried by the support structure – close to the wing stress and spar to fuselage load path theories.

Front drive was another favourite theme, explored by Sason and Mellde. Everyone appreciated, too, that low drag and low rolling resistance would significantly benefit the car. Saab already knew more than any other car maker about all these subjects.

Reaction and Reviews

Of course, the 92 was not perfect. Its front-opening 'suicide' doors had to be changed in 1959; the two-stroke engine was uprated in the 93; and the enclosed front wheel arches, which Sason had included for aerodynamic reasons, tended to foul up with ice, snow and mud.

Despite these minor drawbacks, the 92 was an instant hit.

The Saab's direct competition came from British cars like the Morris Minor – it would be ten years before the front-drive Mini and the low-drag Citroen DS appeared on the scene – and the likes of the Volkswagen Beetle and smaller Peugeots, Fiats, and Renaults, which explored other technical solutions.

A very early road test was carried out on the new Saab by *Motor* magazine. The article, which appeared on 24 August 1949, began as follows:

Total unorthodoxy in the design of a car sets the reviewer a task which is difficult yet exceptionally interesting: difficult because of the lack of normal standards for close comparison, and interesting as revealing the gains and losses which have resulted from new layouts and constructional methods.

The article went on to say, 'The whole layout is so ingenious, both in construction and in detail.' The reporter's conclusion was that 'the Saab 92 is a boldly unconventional design, the further development of which will be watched with great interest'.

Developments

By 1953, the 92 had become the 92B and by 1956 it had been facelifted into the 93, with new front and rear styling, a one-piece windshield, a larger engine and a more international feel. One of the most significant improvements was the change from the two-cylinder transverse-mounted powerplant to a three-cylinder longitudinally installed unit offering 35hp.

Saab made its first exports to the USA in December 1956, with a boat load of 250 93s. Over 6,000 cars a year were soon in production and selling well and Saab was also excelling on the rally scene. From 1960 onwards, the 92/3 and the car it became, the 96, became the core of the Saab legend. Truly people's cars, they still had a degree of class that set them apart.

The culmination of the series was the 96, which had a new rear end, an enlarged rear windscreen and rear side windows, and other major technical revisions. Eventually, a V4 engine design transformed the car, eliminating the unpleasant two-stroke exhaust smoke, and providing an increase of over 30 per cent in power output and much more acceptable performance. The V4 engine, ideal for the 96, was bought in from Ford. It had started life as a US-designed engine under the project code 'Cardinal'

Rolf Mellde

Rolf Mellde, a fanatic of racing and rallying, and an engine expert with an in-depth knowledge of tuning, has an important place in the history of the Swedish motor industry.

Even during his school days, Mellde would draw engines and designs for a turbocharger type of device. He went to work first for a marine engine company and joined Saab's car division in September 1946, where he supported Sason and the front-drive concept. In the 1950s, Mellde won Sweden's toughest rally, the Rikspokalen, and he went on to rally Saab 92s and 93s in many events. He was also the one who recognized the need to ditch the two-stroke engine; he and some others set up a secret research group at Saab in the late 1950s to research four-stroke, four-cylinder engine design.

Mellde came up with the original Sonnet, mostly in his spare time, creating and crafting the car's composite mix of aluminium and fibreglass construction – taken straight from the world of aircraft construction, and unique at the time in a car. Sason styled the body. The design weighed less than 100kg and the drivetrain and suspension hung in aircraft style from a stressed skin steel tub rivetted together. The Sason-styled plastic/fibreglass-based body was then mounted and bonded to the chassis tub. Olle Lindkvist, Gosta Svenson and Olof Olsson worked on the project with Mellde. Saab management loved the car and exhibited it at the 1956 Stockholm motor show, with plans to produce 2,000 cars a year. Several show cars were made, then six early Sonnets, but the planned launch and production never happened. However, the Sonnet sports car idea lived on at Saab.

Mellde's skills in engine design were behind the various projects run in-house at Saab in the late 1950s and early 1960s to create a new four-stroke, four-cylinder engine for the company. It was this work that led to talks with Ricardo and thence to the Triumph affair (see page [00]).

As Technical Director at Saab from 1962 to 1971, he was a key figure in the story of the 99. He later went on to create engineering concepts and prototype cars for Volvo, but he probably remains best known for his work at Saab.

Side view of the Saab 92.

*The final production version of the
Saab 92, late 1949.*

and had found its way into the German-built Ford Taunus model range (a German equivalent to Britain's Cortina). The 60-degree V-angled engine gave 65bhp (DIN) at 1.5 litre capacity, and a four-stroke cycle, with lower emissions. Saab also added all-round disc brakes and trim upgrades.

The 96 sold well in Scandinavia, Europe, Britain and in the USA, where the two-strokes had established a strong following. Safe, fast, comfortable and affordable, the 96 V4 virtually created a new car for Saab, but it was still a one-model company. Sales rocketed, but, with all its eggs in one basket, Saab needed to begin to think in a wider perspective.

SAAB SPORTS CARS

By the mid-1960s, Saab was producing over 30,000 cars per year. Through the skills of Rolf Mellde and Aka Andersson,

and then Eric Carlsson, 'Mr World Rally' of his time, Saab had also become a major name in rallying. With wins in the Monte Carlo, RAC and Safari rallies, the 93–96 models were plastered all over the media, and across Europe. The nimble Saabs even scored rally successes in the USA, against a big-hitting international field.

Saab surprised everyone at this time by turning out a new model. The Sonnet was a fibreglass two-seater sportster, initially a 'one-off' soft top, then a coupe, all based on Saab 93–96 engineering and powerplant. The first Sonnet mixed an aluminium chassis and undertray with a glass-fibre monocoque tub. Rolf Mellde was behind the car, which was unique and years ahead of its time in terms of its composite-type construction. It would take Lotus 40 years to catch up in some respects! The car never made it to series production and the Sonnet badge re-emerged in the Sonnet coupe range. This was a fibre-glass two-seater sports car, which was given V4 power in 1967 and racked up sales in the

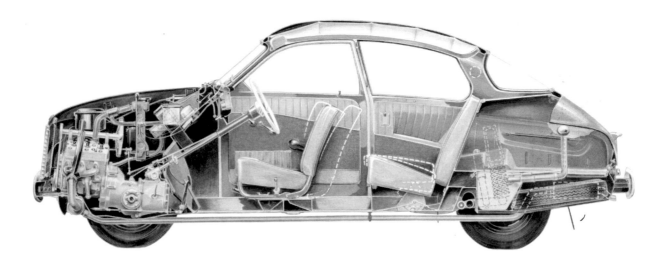

X-ray view of the 96.

Saab 96 – the last of the line that began in 1946.

Marcus Wallenberg

The Wallenberg family of financiers were closely involved with the setting up of Saab and instrumental in the creation of the first Saab car.

Dr Marcus Wallenberg (1899–1982) played a key role in the 1939 amalgamation of the Swedish aviation and engineering firms. When the infant Svenska Aeroplan AB merged with Svenska Jarnvagsverkstaderna (ASJA), Wallenberg emerged via his banking links with ASJA. He joined the board of SAAB in 1939 and made his way to the top, becoming chairman of the merged Saab-Scania group in 1969.

Marcus Wallenberg was the man who drove Saab as a company. According to Sten Gustafsson, later head of Saab-Scania,

Saab-Scania was largely Dr Wallenberg's work. For several decades, he was a living part of the company, giving much of his heart to its activities. Our products today symbolize qualities which he himself appreciated.

Gustafsson went on to point out that it was Marcus Wallenberg who gave people within Saab the time and resources to come up with new ideas.

Former Saab President Tryggve Holm described Wallenberg as an 'enthusiast of vision and energy [who] possessed the will to move mountains'. Wallenberg's own view was that 'those with development potential must be given the environment, surroundings and working conditions to encourage enterprise'. In such an environment, Gunnar Ljungstrom and others were inspired to create the first Saab car, and then the 99, or Project Gudmund.

When a car company has an enthusiast at the helm it usually makes very good cars and Wallenberg proved this theory at Saab.

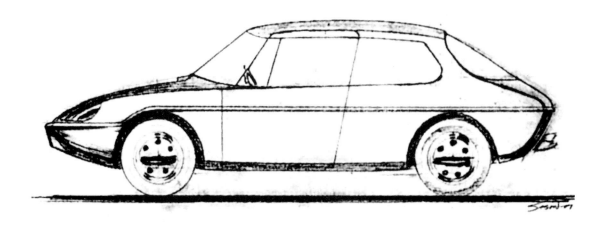

The unpublished 1961 styling proposal of Sixten Sason. Many 99 themes are already apparent. The headlamps and tail were decidedly Italianate, but the concave rear, cabin turret, wedge line and curved windscreen of the production 99, were all there. This sketch led to the conception of the Saab 99.

Sason's drawing of October 1945 – the start of the Saab car look.

USA, where it surprised many with its agility and handling. The company also put its name to a single-seat front-driven racing car – the 'Junior' – and the one-off 'Quantum' sportster.

THE SAAB REPUTATION

The gamble paid off and Saab made its name with its little cars. Its first model – or at least a much-changed version of it – survived in production right through until the early 1980s. The timeless Saab 92 evolved into the capable 96 range over nearly two decades, then the same became true of the 99 and the 900, which developed from 1970 to 1990, and beyond.

The first Saab car set the agenda for the company's philosophy – front-wheel drive, efficient engines, good road-holding and steering feedback, an immensely strong body, and an overall aerodynamics package that was well ahead of its time. And it was created by designers who had never made a car before.

The next step was the very different 99. Suddenly, Saab was not the second-placed Swedish car maker of utilitarian ethos, but an altogether bigger player on the international automotive scene.

2 Project Gudmund

By the early 1960s, Saab knew that it needed a new car. But should it simply replace the 92-96 series with a similar car, tailored to the same market sector, or should it move up a class? From 1962, there was much debate within Saab, and time and money were spent exploring a way of updating the existing car. Facelifted versions were proposed and a couple of prototypes were built. It soon became clear, however, that the future success of the company lay in building a car with a wider appeal for a global market.

On 2 April 1964, the directors of Saab approved plans to develop a completely new car. The project for the new Saab – later to be tagged '99' – was given the name 'Gudmund'.

Work began cautiously, with the new car's engineering – drivetrain and suspension – being secretly installed in a modified Saab 96 nicknamed *Paddan*, or 'toad' in Swedish. Widened by 8in (20cm), Paddan was mounted on an early 99 floorpan and ran around Sweden until the first real 99s appeared.

The prototype 99, with 'Daihatsu' badges and front quarter lights. 'Gudmund' was the name of the day in the Swedish calendar upon which the car was launched.

Late 1965 one of the first bodies is strength tested.

DIFFICULT DECISIONS

In the early 60s, Saab was the only car maker acting on really radical concepts; the 99 was way ahead of most of its contemporaries, with its radical curves and aerodynamics, its enduring modernity and purity of design. Renault, for example, was still producing rear-engined cars for the mass family market. In 1968, the French company launched the 16, a hatchback-styled car; this model, and Saab's 99, were at the forefront of the sea change that took place in car styling from the late 1960s.

In planning the 99, Saab had to assess its future in its home market and, at the same time, look to the worldwide export market. Like every other car maker, its aim was to choose a market sector and tailor a car to it, yet the 99 succeeded in covering several areas of the saloon car market. It competed well in the crossover world of medium-sized saloons of the late 1960s, but it was unlike any of them. Any new car would have to appeal across the market sectors and across the world sales markets – from the USA to Australia, as well as throughout Europe. But Saab could not afford to abandon its core market either, which had been created by the 92-96 series.

The decision on how to proceed was a difficult one. Should a new car have two doors or four, or should it be a hatchback? What size engine should it have? Should it have the square lines that were fashionable at the time, or curves? Was it to be a utility car or a comfort

Saab 99 MkI 1969 (spec set September 1968)

Engine

Type:	Four-cylinder, in-line, single chain-driven OHC; reverse-mounted with flywheel at front. Front drive via gearbox mounted under engine, itself canted at 45 degrees. Five main bearing crankshaft. Pump-driven and splash flow lubrication Enclosed crankcase vent system-cylinder gases air drawn into manifold via valve covers
Block material:	iron
Head material:	aluminium
Cylinders:	four in line at 45-degree angle canted to starboard in plan view
Cooling:	water with fan
Bore and stroke:	3.29in (83.5mm), 3.07in (78.0mm) Capacity (cubic) 1709cc, 104.3cu in displacement
Main bearings:	5
Compression ratio:	9:1
Carburettor:	Stromberg
Max power:	80bhp (DIN) at 5,500rpm
Max torque:	98lb/ft (SAE) at 3,000rpm; 94lb/ft (DIN) at 3,000rpm
Fuel pump:	mech flow
Oil filter:	normal flow
Valve operation:	OHC Camshaft – OHV with chain drive (not belt)

Transmission

Four-speed, chain-driven, located at lower front of engine. Freewheel device.
Hydraulic control sprung clutch actuation

Fourth gear:	0.95:1mph at 1,000rpm: 17.7
Third gear:	1.37:1 11.4
Second gear:	2.04:1 8.2
First gear:	3.22:1 5.2

Synchromesh on all gears

Body

Unitary monocoque with reinforcing beams and bars. Solid, angled-section 2.5mm steel inserts in front windscreen pillars. Rollover cage-type construction. Initially sold as two-door, then four-door

Brakes

Discs all round. Twin diagonal split system. 10.06in discs

Wheels:	15in; 4.5in rims. Tyres 155SSR 15

Suspension

Front:	coil springs and wishbones – independent
Rear:	tube dead axle with trailing longitudinal arms and cross panhard rod, with watts link arms, coil springs; telescopic dampers

Dimensions

Track

Front:	54.7in (1,390mm)
Rear:	55.1in (1,400mm)

Wheelbase:	97.4in (2,473mm)
Weight with petrol and coolant:	2,335lb (1,060kg)
Length:	171.4in (4,354mm)
Width:	66.0in (1,676mm)
Height:	57in (1,450mm)

Other Details

Fuel tank:	steel safety tank in box channel bay; 10.2 gallons capacity
Service interval:	6,000 miles
Ignition timing:	10-degree angle

car? Should it be a thin-gauge European-style steel monocoque structure or a heavy-gauge car to live up to Swedish safety expectations?

Saab wanted to build a car for a world market, but it could not afford to turn its back on the essential ingredients that its Swedish customers had come to expect. A thin-gauge, lightweight car was out of the question. The Swedish winters demanded a thick steel skin, really good rustproofing or undersealing, excellent cabin heating and ventilation, and of course durability and reliability. And the seats would have to be big enough to be comfortable for the average Scandinavian.

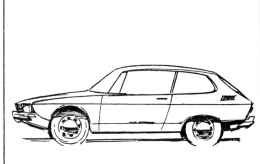

Alternative themes drawn up by Sason for the 99.

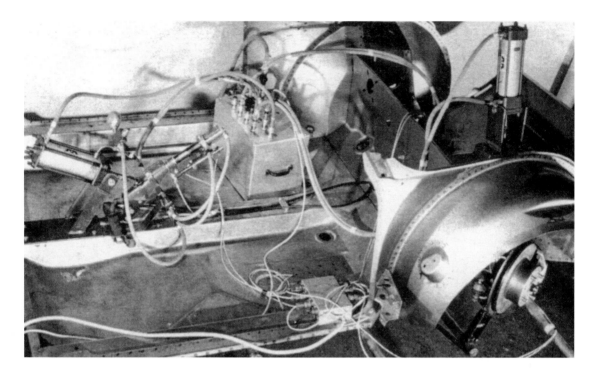

1965 – 99 floorplan and front wheel arches. Note bulkhead and 'A' post mounts on rear of wheelarch.

One thing was certain, however – like all Saabs, the 99 would have front drive and responsive handling. Front drive had proved a definite advantage in Scandinavia's weather and road conditions; rear-driven Volvos lost out in snow and ice to the front-drive Saabs, with their engine weight over the driving wheels.

Clearly, then, the new car would not be a Swedish type of Triumph Herald, or Austin Maxi or Fiat 131, although these cars were competing in the same market sector, as were the first Vauxhall Vivas, Ford Cortinas and other medium-sized family cars. In the end, Saab chose to build a Saab. Its car had appeal beyond the limits of domestic use and it model lifespan turned out to be longer than that of any of its contemporaries.

As early as 1961, Sason had sketched an idea for a larger Saab saloon car. Ljungstrom, Mellde, and other Saab engineers, including Olle Lindqvist, Lars Nilsson, Olle Granland, Sperr Gustaf and a young Bjorn Envall, got together to produce 'Proposal F', which went on to become Project Gudmund. So the shape of the 99 was really born in 1961; it was finalized for tooling in late 1964, but it still looked ultra-modern at the time of its launch three years later.

THE TEAM

Saab personnel resources were relatively tiny at the time; the core design and engineering team numbered around twelve people, as it had for the 92 in 1946. Inevitably, the workforce expanded as

Prototype 99 on rolling road circa 1966.

1967 testing the 99 prototypes.

Project Gudmund proceeded, from 1964 onwards, with over 300 employees working 400,000 man hours on the 99 at its height, but the close-knit family spirit remained. Key people from the Saab aircraft division joined the car division, bringing with them an aeronautical approach. Ragnar Hardmark was one designer who had worked on the Saab 21r and 32 aircraft before directing the Saab 105 jet trainer in 1960.

Marketing and accounting departments exerted less control at Saab than at British Leyland or Ford, for example. Saab's design and development ethos was unusual. Planning meetings were held and directors (notably Svante Holm) guided the development of the car, but the team of designers and engineers enjoyed a rare degree of autonomy. Other car makers in Europe at the time worked in a very different way.

ENGINE PROBLEMS

In 1964, Saab encountered a problem. The new V4 engine, courtesy of a deal with Ford, was due to debut in the 96 from 1966 onwards. This would open up a whole new lease of life for Saab's venerable old charger, but the engine was not relevant to the 99.

Engines had always been a point of discussion within Saab. The two-cylinder, two-stroke that powered the 92 had been derived from the DKW concept. It soon changed to a three-cylinder German-licenced unit, and from transverse to

Early 99 with extra grille vents circa 1970.

lengthwise installation. Many years later, long after Mellde had urged Saab to adopt the four-cylinder engine and transform its cars, the Ford V4 found its way under the same bonnet.

What would power the new car? There was confidence that the Saab team would come up with a finely engineered car, but the car needed a new engine – and Saab did not have one. The costs and resources involved in coming up with its own new power unit would have meant a delay. Saab could not afford to get it wrong or to take too huge a gamble.

In the early 1960s, Rolf Mellde, Per Gillbrand and Karl Rosenqvist had been exploring among themselves a 1.2-litre four-cylinder powerplant idea for Saab. Their work had been carried out in liaison with British engine designers Ricardo, which was working on engine designs for Triumph and its new small to medium-sized car, the Dolomite. To save time and money, Saab talked to Ricardo and then high-level contact between Saab and Standard (or Triumph) led to an agreement to share the engine – albeit in different states of technical specification. The 1.5-litre unit was uprated to 1709cc for both companies.

The 1.7-litre engine had to be inclined at an angle of 45 degrees to fit under the bonnet, partly because it formed half of the V8 engine created by Triumph for its Stag. The Triumph versions of the four-cylinder engine (intended for the Dolomite model) had a few teething problems that Saab naturally wanted to sidestep. There were pressure spots on the cylinder head – to block mounts even in the revised, but still British-built, Saab version – giving rise to gasket effects. Saab re-engineered the engine for its own purposes, changing the gasket and head mounting. (The V8 version did go on to suffer long-term reliability problems when used in the Triumph Stag.)

Saab had agreed to take up to 50,000 British-built engines a year and publicly announced that its new car would have a Triumph-derived engine, built in England. The early 99s appeared with this engine. Iron blocked with an alloy head and a 1709cc 87bhp (DIN) capacity, it was smooth and quiet, but not particularly economical. The Saab version also placed the clutch and gearbox at the front of the engine, low down, providing excellent cooling. It was also 'back to front', according to the British press!

On Project Gudmund, engine work came first, followed by the body concepts. The ideas were then actioned into a car project by the board, in a reversal of the normal process.

STYLING AND SAFETY

Project Gudmund had to signify a move up for Saab and, for its time, the 99 was extremely advanced in terms of engineering and design. It remained safe many years after its launch, while other manufacturers caught up, and built some crash strength into their cars. Like the 92, the car had double-skinned, heavy-gauge panels and reinforced pillars.

The styling was highly advanced. The car had a very 'clean' look, without any excess of chrome ornamentation, or bulbous, hard-to-weld panels. It was curved, but it was also simple and timeless. It was also totally different from the Volvo 142 and 144 offered by its nearest home-grown competitor.

The Saab's seats were especially comfortable, with an early and rather crude system of height adjustment. There was rear cabin heating. The large wheels and front-drive handling, with communicative steering and pedal forces, made it a real driver's car. Only an initial lack of urge marked it down, and that was soon rectified.

3 Saab 99 – Styling Standpoint

We had real trouble with that one. Sixteen was up all night trying to get the back end right. I was just the new boy, the assistant. What he really wanted was an Alfa-style glassed-in rear boot – a sort of hatchback coupe. It's funny how years later we got closer to his original idea with the three-door 99 body shell. He was never really happy with the original idea for the rear end of the 99, and it gave us lots of aerodynamic problems, but we solved them in the end and the rear view grew on you.

Bjorn Envall

EARLY SKETCHES

Eighteen-year-old Bjorn Envall began at Saab in 1960 as studio junior, and rose to Head of Design in the 1970s and 80s. During the 99 project, Envall was fortunate enough to be able to observe Sason as the design genius sketched and sketched, searching for a theme for the 99. Because of Sason's ill health, the result of an air crash, Envall even had a hand in the final details of the 99, notably the front and rear lamp and grille designs.

When Saab decided to launch a completely new car, more advanced than the 92-96 series cars, much work had already been done. The early 92 and 93 series cars were well styled, but they were not modern. Saab needed to be bold and the 99 was nothing like its competitors, such as the Morris Oxford and the Ford Cortina, which recalled pre-war design. Only the Renault 16 and the Pininfarina shapes of the time hinted at a more aerodynamic world in this market sector. Only the 99 was still in production two decades later.

The first sketches for the 99, dating from 1961, reveal another aspect of Sason's futuristic vision – the 'cab-forward' design – with the cabin reaching forward in order to create more space. (The style became very popular in the 1990s.) Sason's drawings also showed his admiration of American styling themes. He liked wedged bodies, shovel noses and curved lines, with tapered fronts and rears. The concave rear, and its expensive wraparound rear windscreen, with a touch of Alfa Romeo, suggests a hatchback – some time before such designs came to the fore. The later Michelotti-styled Triumph cars had a rear windscreen and C pillar design that was not dissimilar. The front lights and undertray are Citroenesque, in the style of the slant-front revised DS – except that they were drawn years before that DS was launched, in 1967. Saab rejected Sason's glazed-in nose as too adventurous for its car. Saab may not have been looking for sporty styles such as these, but the basic lines of the 99 are there.

There was debate over the front-end styling too. To keep the conservatives happy, some of Sason's early sketches had incorporated contemporary round headlamps and chromed-up 'mouth' front grilles. Sason's square-headlamped, faired-in nose won the day, however (although versions for the American market ended up with round headlamps, because of US law).

Bjorn Envall: Stylish Swede

At the age of 18, design student Bjorn Envall sent Sixten Sason a portfolio of sketches. Sason contacted Envall, interviewed him and took him on straight away as the design office junior.
Sason and Envall got on well and the young designer was allowed to have a major input into his senior's projects from early on in his career. He was closely involved in the shaping of the 99, and Sason's ill health meant that Envall actually ended up adding the final styling details to the front and rear of the car. He also had a hand in the 'Katherina' targa-topped coupe. Envall developed a good feel for what was wanted.

Envall spent time with Opel in Germany before returning to head Saab's design department. He oversaw the maturing of the 99, the advent of the Combi Coupe and the styling of the 900 (most notably, the creation of the convertible), and outlined the shape of the revised GM 900 before his departure from Saab. He also put his name to the extraordinary Saab EV1 show car, a mix of pure Saab styling themes with a dose of future vision – certainly not a retro pastiche, but an accomplished piece of automotive sculpture.

Under Sason, Envall learned to design the whole body package and not just to clothe a chassis with a styled body. EV1 impressively demonstrated his learning and his talent.
After leaving Saab, Bjorn Envall set up his own company and ventured into product design. He remains a household name in Scandinavian design.

Bjorn Envall, Saab's styling chief after Sason.

AHEAD OF ITS TIME

The 99 was the first truly wedge-shaped car, with a low, narrow front and rising body line. It featured a curved, dart-nosed front panel rising into a taut cabin shape. The bonnet line ran through to the rear end and flicked up to form the shape of the rear side windows – an early 'graphical window' treatmen, as the designers call it. It had a reverse aerofoil-section nose (most apparent when the car is seen with its bumpers removed), which gave good down force and directed the under-car airflow. The 99 also had DRG – 'down-the-road graphic' – a design term for the strength of a car's stance and the way light is caught and highlighted by its styling themes.

The door frames overlapped the wind-screen pillars. Most other cars of the time had windscreen pillars that divided the door frame from the windscreen, all edged with less than aerodynamic thick rubber trims. In the 99, Sason predicted today's overlapping door frames and wrapped the front-door window frame over the wind-screen pillar. The triangular-section rein-forced pillar hid behind the door frame, giving a much thinner and smoother join between the screen and side panels. The thinness of the pillar area aided visibility; the benefits of this were enhanced by placing the narrowest edges of the pillars towards the driver, allowing a wider field of vision. Saab was also one of the first to dispense with front-window quarter lights, at a time when these appeared, chrome-trimmed, on virtually every new car. Most car makers were to keep such quarter lights for another ten years.

Some considered that the rear of the car had a sculptural rump or 'bottom', perhaps reflecting Sason's interest as an artist in the female form.

All in all, the design of the 99 was time-less and enduring. It was a genuine design statement; at its launch, it was both leading edge and acceptable.

AERODYNAMICS

Before Sason's time, Paul Jaray was the only car designer to explore aerodynamics as part of a total package. Few other car makers built clay bucks and tuned them in wind tunnels, as Saab did in 1965. As with the 92 in 1947, superb aerodynamics were a hallmark of the 99. The car was a fine testament to Saab's pioneering work in the area.

The rear end of the 99 was most unusual at the time, featuring a concave, swept bootline that swung down in a clean arc from the top of the roof. It was the first time such a style had been used, although it would appear later on the Renault 12, the Ford Zodiac and the Hillman Avenger.

The design tied down the point of air-flow separation over the car's roof and gave the designers a chance to stabilize the critical separation point (or CSP). The airflow over the car was tuned to break at the top of the rear windscreen and then tumble inwards and downwards over the rear screen and boot. Ideally, the airflow is kept attached as far back and as far down the rear of a car as possible, but airflow does not bend without breaking and it is much better deliberately to create its break-up moment, rather than have a huge envelope of drag created behind the car. Fine engineering in the 99 deliberately triggered the airflow break and then controlled the wake turbulence.

The later three-door design moved towards a coupe-style rear end, which aided airflow attachment. (True coupes and fastbacks keep their airflow attached down to the lip of the boot or hatch lid.) The 99 was effectively making the best of the compromise that a booted 'three-box' type of design forced upon the aerodynamicist.

The clamshell bonnet used on the 99 was unusual, having been seen only at BMW. The shape of the Saab's windscreen was totally unique for a production car – only the Lancia Stratos had a more curved version. To ensure good airflow and to reduce the pressure wave bubble that builds up in front of most flat windscreens, Sason came up with a 'beetle-browed turret'. The super-curved windscreen allowed the air to split and sweep around the front of the car with minimum turbulence.

The 99 achieved a remarkable drag co-efficient (CD) figure of 0.37 in 1967. Only the Citroen DS could match it. At the time, most cars had drag figures of at least 0.45 and many were as high as 0.50; the average CD figure did not drop to 0.35 until the late 1980s. The 99's dart-like front, curved windscreen, domed roof, sharp rear flanks, and undertray all kept the airflow attached and as low in turbulence as possible. The 99's cross-sectional frontal drag figure (CDA) was good, too, because of the curved front windscreen.

INTERIOR

The 99's original interior was aircraft-inspired. It had a dashboard 'coaming' that ran along the fascia top and into the front-door trims at window-ledge height. The 96-style instruments, with their innovative green back lighting, were cowled and clearly presented and grouped. The vast curve of the windscreen also gave the car its table-top type upper fascia area, which stretched forwards by over a foot to the furthest point of the windscreen. In a crash, the heads of the front-seat occupants were a long way from the windscreen and impact area.

The seats were orthopaedically designed. Large and well shaped, with long squabs to provide good leg support for the taller-than-average Scandinavians, they offered a new standard in comfort for motorists outside Sweden.

REACTIONS

At the launch of the 99, *Motor* magazine hoped that the car would be 'avidly digested not only by Saab fans but by anyone with up to £1,500 to spend on a family holdall'. The reviewer went on to say:

> Perhaps we could venture to suggest that some of the industry's chief engineers and body men take a look, too, because in several detail ways – and even in certain aspects of its styling – the 99 is something of a trendsetter that we much admire.

According to *CAR* magazine, the 99 – just a basic family car, after all – was 'a piece of carefully considered industrial design'.

COMPROMISES AND ALTERATIONS

Although the production car could not incorporate everything that Sason wanted in terms of stylistic advancement, his original themes were almost all there. The curved screen, clamshell bonnet, rising window line and taught C pillar are became familiar styling motifs, repeated on later Saabs, right up to the 9-5.

At its launch, the 99 was truly a fresh face on the world scene of car design and. Surprisingly, some members of the Swedish motoring press thought that the car looked a bit tame. They had been conditioned into expecting something as advanced as the 92 of 1949. For once,

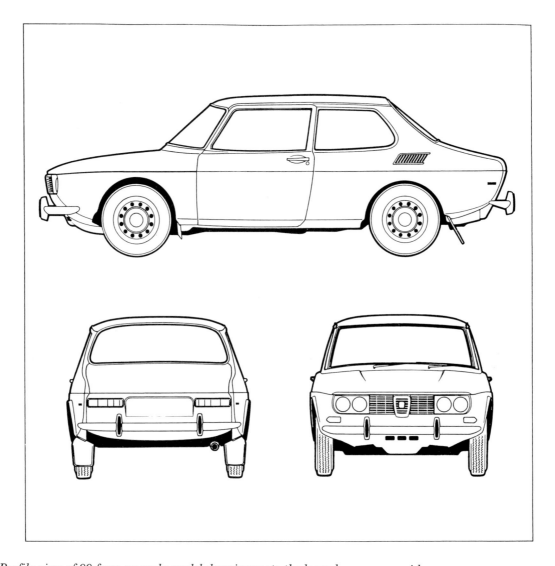

Profile view of 99 from an early model drawing; note the large bumper over-riders.

however, a touch of compromise seemed to have worked. The 99 was just what Saab needed for its survival, and it was to have a long life, with just a few styling tweaks.

The early cars had chrome bumpers and a decidedly Italianate look around the front grille and lamps. Less than three years into the life of the car, as early as 1971, the 99's styling was subtly yet strongly altered. Without making any tooling changes – other than minor alterations to the front bumper valance – Bjorn Envall (who had trained under Sason) took the original 1960s-style Sason front, and updated it. In doing so, he introduced a Saab look that has endured to this day. Rubber bumpers and the hallmark rearward-curved side repeater/indicator shape were grafted on. Sason's delicate front end – reminiscent of 1960s Alfa and Lancia themes – suddenly became stronger and bolder. The purity of Sason's original arrow-shaped front had been diluted a little, but the new design was certainly more modern.

The modification significantly altered the character of the 99. Overnight, it left the 1960s behind, and became a car of the 1970s. The difference between the two cars is startling. The wider frontal area – larger indicator units placed at the top corners of the front wings – also cased some initial aerodynamic turbulence. This was tuned out by alterations to the shape of the new indicator lens mouldings.

In the 1970s, a corporate grille was designed for Saab. It blended into the 99, but it made its real mark on the 900. The pentangle-ended oblong design actually first saw the light of day on the 1967 US market Sonnet.

Originally available with only two doors, the 99 was planned with four doors as far back as 1964. Two extra rear doors were introduced in 1970 and the original style only needed to be slightly altered in order to incorporate them. If anything, the strength of the shape of the C pillar became even more pronounced in the four-door shape.

The rear lamps were also altered at this time, but the simple, stylish steel wheels, with their circular holes and chrome centres, were left untouched.

4   Strength and Safety

Go Swift, Go Safe, Go Saab
(Saab publicity slogan of the 1960s)

SAFETY CONCERNS

The Saab car company has always shown an extraordinary dedication to – some say an obsession with – safety, and many lives have been saved by its designs. According to all international crash safety organizations, drivers are much more likely to survive a crash in a Saab than in many other makes of car. And this has been the case since the 1950s and the days of the 92-96 series. Saab had a crash safety centre of advanced thinking years before many other car makers; today, along with its closest rival Volvo, Saab leads the field in this area. After its launch, the Saab 99 won the Don safety trophy in the UK, and many other awards have followed since.

Today, safety is an acknowledged selling point for a car, but there was a time when buyers were simply not interested. Volvo fitted safety belts as standard and furthered the 'safety cell' concept, as did Mercedes-Benz, but many car makers paid little attention to crash safety. Saab was different. Under Olle Lindqvist, Saab's main body stress engineer, and later under senior safety engineer Lars Nilsson, the 99 and the 900 far exceeded all known safety standards.

At one time, the motoring press accused Volvo of creating cars that were crash-proof, but of placing less emphasis on avoiding a crash in the first place. It was the difference between 'passive' and 'active' safety. Saab put the emphasis on the benefits of front-drive handling, but excelled in both areas of safety. It pioneered side-impact protection way back in 1972, fitting sturdy door beams into the doors of the 99. In 1970, it offered proper headlamp washers with lens wipers – a major contribution to road safety.

SAFE CONSTRUCTION

Steel

The legacy of the first Saabs was structural integrity and in-built reinforcements. The 92 and the 99 were made of low-carbon, high-quality grade British steel. Steel beams and cross-members reinforced the cabin. Many of the panels – notably the rear side body panels – were constructed of steel that was 0.047in thick. The steel was in places nearly twice as thick as the steel used on some rivals' cars, and thicker in gauge than the steel used on the average car by approximately 20 per cent. Building on the 92-96 designs, the 99 had a very strong body that was way ahead of its competitors in the safety stakes. The car had a high torsional stiffness rating (over 5,000lb/ft/sq in) – in its advertisements for the 99, Saab referred to the car's 'steel-basket' construction. In 1975, Mel Nichols at *CAR* magazine called the 99's body strength 'incredible'.

Front and Rear End

The front of the car – inner wings, wheel arches and bulkhead – was a one-piece construction unit to which the screen pillars, floor and side panels were welded. Most panels were large and close-welded, giving extra rigidity. The panels, from the B posts back to the edge of the rear wings, were pressed as a single piece, to ensure maximum strength. Underneath the outer monocoque skin, the 99 had chassis struts that connected the B pillars to the rear wheel arches and then continued back in another strut from the wheel arch down through the rear wings. This gave the car a sub-chassis element and made it stronger than the usual hollow monocoque. This method of construction – allied to the steel-basket passenger-cage construction – made the car resist twist by up to 30 per cent more than other contemporary designs.

It was normal at the time to concentrate all the car's strength in two beams pro-truding from the centre of the engine bay. Many car makers used this 'battering-ram' type of front end in order to pass head-on crash tests, but it failed to work in an off-set or angled front impact. The 99 had a widely spaced front section, with impact structures in each of the front wings, leading back to massive steel wheel-arch housings. Indeed, the housings and front-wing crowns were so strong that they actually had to be weakened a decade later in one or two areas for the 900, in order to provide more 'crushability' and meet new impact legislation.

At the rear, the fuel tank was ahead of the axle. In the 1970s and 80s, other car makers regretted not adopting this layout, when their own exposed fuel tanks caused a furore.

Beyond the axle, a three-pronged chassis fork member spread out towards

X-ray view of 99 two-door saloon; note the A post beams running into the front wheel arch. The thick box section sills and floor cross beams are also evident.

the rear bumper, giving load strength and a load path for any rear-end impact. Crash forces were carried into the C pillar and lower chassis, and energy was dissipated.

Rollover Protection

Under the curved windscreen, there was a massive, armour-plated bulkhead, which was tied into the windscreen pillars. The pillars were unique in design terms – incredibly rigid and almost solid at one angle. Most car roof pillars consist of a hollow section of multiple pressings of thin sheet steel, spot-welded together and linked into the overall structure. They have an inherent strength, but are surprisingly flimsy when isolated. The Saab windscreen pillars defied convention. They were made of angle-section 2.5mm steel sandwiched into a triangular beam of unprecedented strength, and

resisted twist to a far greater degree than the pillars of most other cars. As a result, the Saab 99 and 900 boasted roof strength far beyond legislative demands. If they were turned over, it was rare to see the roof crushed.

On the 99, the pillars were seated into the bottom of the front wheel arches and rebated back against the oversize sill box and heavy-gauge doors. This construction assured maximum possible rollover protection and gave frontal-impact penetration or resistance characteristics that were much better than normal. In a crash, the 'soft' nose on the 99 absorbed the first impact, then the front end resisted harder the further back the crash energy comes.

In response to new American crash tests in the early 1980, the 900 was given extra length in the wheelbase, and in the forward nose, providing more crush zone up front. The lower anchoring point of the wheel

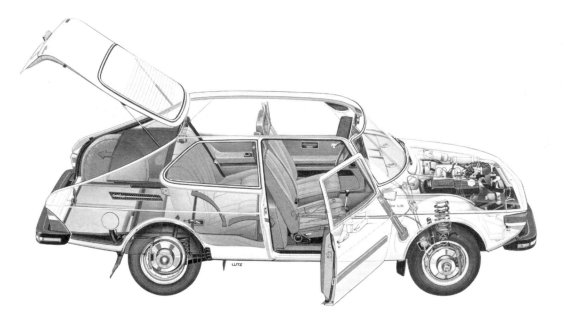

X-ray view of the three-door Combi Coupé body shell.

Drop test – the 99 is dropped on its roof from a height of 8ft (2.4m). The windscreen pillars remain unbuckled and the roof stays upright. Such rollover protection was rare in the 1960s.

The 99 undergoing head-on frontal-impact testing at 30mph in 1966. The cabin area remains intact, doors undamaged and sills straight, with little rearwards intrusion towards the cabin. Crash safety is a Saab hallmark.

X-ray view of the 900.

arches had to be moved forwards and the 'sandwiched' windscreen pillars had to be cut off at the scuttle and welded into the bulkhead or firewall.

In 1983, a collision with a wandering elk caused the death of a Saab director in a 900, so Saab further reinforced the 900's windscreen pillar tie-down points with some extra flanges and sections. The 'elk test' is still used by Saab for all its new cars, benefiting drivers wherever they are in the world.

Most cars at the time had to have the windscreen firmly sealed, bonded or channelled into the surround frame, to stop it popping out in the event of a crash, which would twist the roof pillars. The 99's roof pillars moved so little in a crash that the front windscreen could be held in place just by its rubber trim.

On the 99, the B and C posts – the other roof pillars behind the windscreen posts – were also heavy gauge, contributing to the rollover protection. The thick and heavy doors featured a turned-under bottom that extended several inches into the floorpan to rebate up against massive box-section inset sill members.

From 1972, the 99 came with a unique fibreglass padded roof lining – another industry first. This padded interlayer gave better head protection to occupants in the event of a rollover. Constant neck protection was provided by very strong head restraints, always a Saab hallmark.

RESEARCH AND REFINEMENTS

Saab engineers often visited the sites of crashes involving their cars, in order to learn what lessons they could and consider any refinements that could be made. In the 1980s, for example, the aftermath of a head-on crash between a Saab 99 and a similar-sized saloon from British Leyland was a sobering sight. The Saab had crumpled up to the windscreen, but the sills, doors and roof remained intact – giving vital survival space for the occupants. The other car simply folded backwards into the cabin as the floorpan and roof folded up, trapping the occupants.

The 900 further enhanced the 99's already good safety standards with its extra crush zone length and padding. It featured a collapsible steering column refinement and extra weld points, and a special energy-absorbing steering wheel debuted on it in 1979. The 99 also introduced the split diagonal braking system at Saab. The wishbone front suspension once again put the emphasis on handling.

In the 1970s, as a result of investigations into real-life accidents, Saab added wide moulded armrests to the door trims of the 99. The engineers had found that side-impact intrusion was causing a high rate of injury, and devised a special padded door trim, with impact-absorbing armrests that collapsed on crushing to protect the occupants' hips and upper torso. Lars Nilsson oversaw these important developments.

5   The 99 Unveiled

The 99 was certainly a people's car, but it also had character and it was not long before it became a luxury-trimmed, higher-powered saloon with sporting ambitions. It created a niche of its own in the mid-range, but it also appealed to the market on either side of that sector.

At the time of the 99's development, Saab was under the stewardship of Tryggve Holm, alongside Svante Holm, who handed over the running of the company to Curt Mileikowsky in 1967. The Wallenbergs were still in force at board level. Saab was still a small company with limited resources. Sason and his young assistant Bjorn Envall toiled away trying to find a form that fitted the function, while Ljungstrom, Mellde and their engineers worked on drafting the basics of the technical specification. As with the 92, the team did what they knew was best – creating a Saab. Fortunately, they had got into the habit of getting things near the mark at the first or second attempt.

A MODERN CAR

In every sense, the new Saab was modern – in terms of styling, engineering, cabin design and trim. Front drive was a must, as were safety, durability and an interior of

A very early (late 1967) car, with rear-view mirror mounted on the front wing.

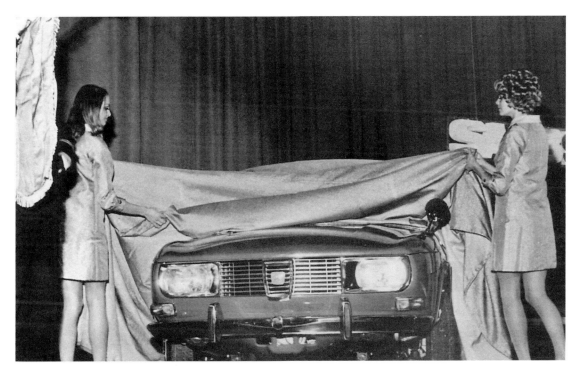

The new 99 unveiled in Stockholm on 22 November 1976.

This is the early four-door 99 – with chrome bumpers and 'nostril'-style grille vents. Such cars are now extremely rare.

The purity and modernity of the Sason lines are shown in a 1968 launch publicity shot of the early 99, with the Saab Viggen fighter aircraft behind it.

carefully designed quality. The 99 boasted folding rear seats with the collapsing rear backrest creating a massive, flat cargo area 5ft 9in (1.75m) long, accessed via the boot or the front side doors. With the front seats forward, it was even possible to stretch out and sleep in the 99 – a feature that was typical of the men at Saab and found favour with many owners. Over-engineering went into the front driveshafts and their CV joints, which lasted for up to double the mileage of the joints on other front-driven cars.

Saab gave the car's rear cabin heating ducts and extractor vents in the rear wings to get rid of stale air. It had a unique, air-heated rear windscreen demister. It seated four in good comfort, and five with ease (although taller Scandinavians probably felt more comfortable with just two in the rear).

PRE-PRODUCTION TESTING AND LAUNCH

The 99 was a carefully thought-out car, the eventual result of 400,000 man hours of design, engineering and production work. Pre-production testing was extensive and comprehensive.

The 99 had 15in wheels and a lot of weight to haul around, so Saab wanted to test its front-drive components thoroughly

Model Milestones

Note: model year changes usually announced September/October of preceding year

Late 1967:	Saab 99 two-door launch model. 1709cc Triumph-built engine. UK sales begin late summer 1969
Late 1969:	rare early four-door cars with original dashboard but larger 1854cc engine and grille changes
Spring 1970:	major dashboard changes and revised grille
Late 1970:	four-door body shell with 1854cc engine and 1.85-litre badges, designated 99CM4
Late 1971:	revised front styling, with rubber bumpers. Two-door shell designated 99CM2. Wide chrome strips on rubber bumpers
Early 1972:	autobox launched with injection engine, designated 99LEA4
Late 1972:	Swedish-made 1985cc engine debuts, designated 99LCM2 and 99LCM4/99LEA
Late 1973:	99 EMS two-door shell, designated 99LEA4
Late 1974:	99 EMS updated with black vinyl roof and USA trim changes. Combi three-door body shell, designated 99LCM3
Late 1974:	five-door Combi shell, designated 99LCM5
Spring 1975:	99LEA4 autobox discontinued. 99LCA4 auto carb introduced
Late 1975:	luxury GLE range debuts. Power steering on GL trim. Chrome strips on rubber bumpers narrowed, then deleted
Late 1976:	styling revisions, new rear lamps and frontal treatment. First three-door with Turbo development shells, 100 cars
1976–85:	99 model development and Turbo cars
Late 1977:	front indicator lamps made larger, new rear lamps on saloons, side mouldings added
Late 1978:	base model extended in L trim from two-door shell to three-door. EMS as Combi three-door coupe in USA. Three-door EMS with silver paint and black spoilers/trim for other markets
Late 1979:	revised rear axle, new wheel design, changes to front suspension geometry. 99 super model as four-door for Norway. Late model 99s for UK due to late launch of RHD 900 in UK market
1980:	900 trim upgrades across slimmed-down 99 range. Dechroming with black trim. 900 interior and seat patterns adopted
Spring 1980:	Turbo models debut
1981–84:	revised H-series engine. Trim upgrades, special one-offs and model run-out. Five-speed gearbox on 99 Turbo in selected markets. Extra batch of 99 Turbo two-door MkIIs for UK market. Numbers of 400/600/800 quoted. Mostly in red

1969 US market model 99, with round headlamps and optional Art Deco-style headrests, unique at the time.

for durabilty and longevity. Preventing driveshaft failures was important for Saab's reputation and the 99 had permanently lubricated drive joints. Fifty prototypes were made and badged up as Japanese Daihatsus, to disguise them from press and public. Many were destroyed in testing, including one that crashed inside the Saab facility during CV joint and driveshaft trials. Careering into a brick wall, it became the first 99 to be written off by accident.

In order to escape the spy photographers of the press, and to cover as many miles as possible, Saab took the development cars to Northern Finland. For a wider variety of road surfaces and conditions, the 99 was also taken to Eastern Europe, where the suspension settings, sealing, dri-

vetrain and steering angles were honed. During hundreds of thousands of 'proving' miles, the production cars threw up no serious surprises.

The early 99s had front quarter lights, but these were removed prior to series production.

Even after the design was set, Saab refused to let the car out on the market. Almost a year was spent tweaking early pre-production cars that had been placed into the hands of a chosen group of Saab owners. Their feedback was to prove very useful in helping the 99 enter service with as few teething problems as possible.

The new car was launched to the world on Wednesday 22 November 1967 in Stockholm, but it would be yet another year before it was put into mass series production.

In November 1967, the new Saab car – upon which the company's future lay – finally took to the roads. Saab engineers and selected customers carried out proving trials over all kinds of Swedish road surfaces, and their feedback proved invaluable. By late 1968, after pre-production sampling, the new 99 was ready for lift-off for the 1969 model year. It was an immediate hit across Scandinavia, selling 19,411 and achieving fifth place in the car market for 1969. Despite Saab's geographical isolation, it caused a stir in Great Britain too, perhaps because the early model had a British engine. Scottish crofters and hill farmers of northern and western England found the 99 ideal; the unique fold-down seat gave 23 square feet for the carrying of unusual cargo, even sheep!

The 99's handling was expertly tuned mild front-drive understeer with no undesirable 'lift-off' effects. All-round coil springs with double front wishbones gave excellent control and a low c.g. and roll centres. At the time of the 99's design, multi-link suspension design was the preserve of sports and racing cars. (Indeed, Honda was to get excited about such a suspension set-up thirty years later.) Saab even built a degree of self-steer into the rear suspension design.

In order to meet production numbers for the new car and the revised V4-powered 96, Saab had to open up every avenue of factory space. In 1969, Saab became Saab-Scania Aktiebolaget, in a merger between Saab AB and Scania Vabis AB. Car production was then centred on Södertälje, south of Stockholm, and production capacity was brought in from all over Sweden, notably from plants in Linköping, Kristenhamn and Nykoping.

Saab also had a new factory venture with the Finnish firm Valmet OY. In 1969, the company began making cars in Finland at Uusikaupunki on the Baltic coast. In 1971, the Finnish factory assembled 7,781 99 models.

In 1970, total car production at Saab was 73,982 cars, 29,755 of which were early-model 99s. The 500,000th Saab car to be made since the firm's inception was a 99.

TEETHING PROBLEMS AND NEGATIVE REACTIONS

Negative comments from the motoring press concerned the 99's acceleration and rather heavy, non-assisted steering, and its 'notchy' or 'recalcitrant' gearbox, with its rather stiff gear changes. Twenty years later, a 900 was tested by a certain British motoring magazine, and the same gearbox was even described as 'diabolical'. The gearbox was to become one of few real demerits on the 99 and 900; even after the 99 years had passed, the original gearbox design continued to cause problems on some cars. Many Saab experts believed that driving style and temperature affected the gearbox's behaviour. The fact was that gear changes could not be rushed, and the problem was less prevalent with slow changes.

Technical changes were made to the gearbox bearings and strength was increased over the years. Saab also added extra air inlets on the front panel to cool the gearbox, but failures still seemed to be random. A rattly gearbox could go on for ever, but occasionally it would explode and shatter its cast housing – a rare but significant failure.

Oil leaks were a problem on early-build cars, but the factory soon tightened up on this.

The steering issue became a contentious one. On thin tyres pumped up to 30lb or more, on packed Scandinavian snow and ice, the steering lightened. On unfrozen

The original interior, with optional headrests.

roads, on wider tryes with lower inflation and a larger 'footprint', the steering was heavy, particularly at parking speeds. Saab took its time to address the problem, although the revised rack on the EMS model of 1972 helped. In the 1980s, some owners tried to install power steering from the 900 in their 99s.

1968: EARLY CARS

The first press cars came in a strong shade of red called Toreador, a colour that complemented the car's lines well and featured in most of the publicity. The car was also available in white, blue, a traditional Saab green, black and a light tan or taupe. Early brochures also referred to a colour called Silversand, seen later on the EMS.

Early Features

Some features on the early cars were very short-lived and had been changed by the start of the 1970 model year (at Saab, at the end of August/beginning of September). Passenger and driver's seats were height-adjustable; the passenger seat height adjustment was deleted for 1970. The first cars had a horn stalk, but within one year the horn actuation had been moved to the steering-wheel pad. The bonnet-release handle was from the V4, as were the universal joints on the driveshafts. The first few hundred 99s had a '99' badge on the dashboard. This was subsequently removed and the clock from the 96 model was inserted into the space. Again, by the time the 1970 model year had come around, these items had been changed to dedicated 99 model designs.

The original pressed steel dashboard with 'coaming' design and Saab 96 clock.

Another sign of early times was the ergonomically positioned ashtray, on the top of the dashboard, near the steering wheel, requiring minimal movement from the driver. There was also an angled cigarette holder, which put the cigarette conveniently at the driver's disposal.

Interior

Most of the early cars had a black-trimmed interior with seats in a material called 'nylon tricot'. Blue cars came with blue seats and trim, while the black cars came with grey seats and trim in a very rare 'velour velvet' material. Grey carpet was standard. Interestingly, the original 1968 Saab 99 brochure shows a colour photograph of a 99 with bright red seats and carpets, yet it is not mentioned in the brochures until 1971. Seat trim was a ribbed synthetic cloth, although the early brochures showed an alternative black vinyl. Both front seats had cam roller two-position height adjustment, which was very rare at the time. Early cars also had air-heated rear windscreens, later changed to electric elements.

At first, the cars had no headrests, but soon Saab offered the upright, open, tennis-racket style head restraints. They were standard fit on the early USA-spec 99s and then were found on many of the cars for the northern European markets, but were offered only as an optional extra in the UK. Saab stuck with these headrests until the high-backed seats debuted.

The early cars also had the aircraft-style 'coaming' interior, with side-door trims arced upwards and inwards to meet the fascia at each edge. There was a real feel of being in a cockpit. The original fascia pressing was completely changed for the 1971 model year, when a deeper, more modern design was introduced. Early cars had a shallow, full-width dashboard in matt black with a dividing chrome strip running across the passenger side to link up with the three instrument dials and a 96-style clock. A pleated padded knee roll extended downwards below this shallow dashboard. On the passenger sides, a glovebox and grab handle ended in a swivel vent.

The early interiors had chrome highlights on fittings and instruments, some of which came from the 94-96 model. The chrome-rimmed clock was centrally mounted on the fascia, and there was a Saab logo beneath the sliding heater controls. The freewheel control knob (see below) could be found at the leading edge of the console between the seats, next to the short, stubby gear lever.

Saab 99: Trim and Spec Evolution 1969–84 (90 Model, 1985–87)

Saab 99 revealed November 1967; pre-production series cars during 1968

Model year 1969
Chassis numbers 99 001001-99 014259
1709cc 80hp DIN
Four-speed gearbox with freewheel capacity. Chrome trim and bumpers. Early dashboard with coaming. Two-door only. Low-level indicator units

Model year 1970
First Finnish-built cars. Chassis numbers 99 600006-90 601640
1.85-litre engine with fuel injection on autobox cars, three-speed. Four-door saloon added to range. Extra engine mounting point, new drive joints

Model year 1971
Larger 1.85-litre engine 87hp DIN across range, 95hp DIN injection models. Base model with 1.7 manual drivetrain only.
Additions included: headlamp wash wipe, new instruments and panel. Large brake vacuum assistance

Model year 1972
99 EMS launched
1.85 engine now manual or auto
Range updates included: heated seats, new wheel design, rubber bumpers (impact type), revised front-corner styling and lights
Note: from February 1972, redesigned Swedish version of original engine, 110hp DIN

Model year 1973
Addition of side-impact beams in doors (an industry first)
Smaller engines on lower trim models. New moulded roof lining across range

Model year 1974
First of Belgian-assembled cars. Chassis numbers 99 74 70 000001-99 74 70 04096
Two main engine options for world market, 1.85 and 2.0 litre
1974 cars with new high-backed seat design with integral headrests
Three-door body shell debuts as Combi Coupe in 1974. 52 cu ft of cargo-carrying space with seats folded

Model year 1975
Base model upgraded to 100hp DIN with full-impact bumpers and trim
Chassis improvements, larger fuel tank, electrical upgrades to 55 amp
Rare three-door Combi shell with panelled side window as van: general chassis improvements, larger fuel tank, new grille. Fuel-injected engine output rises to 118hp DIN. Twin-carb model as three-door 99L

Model year 1976
Improved spec, new instruments. Five-door Combi body shell launched with 'opera' side windows at rear
GL and GLE trim created, with luxury finish, rear-seat headrests, etc
EMS spec upgraded

Model year 1977
First turbo-engined 99s, numbered 900-999
Mostly three-door. New lamps and grille across range. Larger rear lights. Side mouldings and trim strip changes across range

Model year 1978
Rare EMS-Turbo badged cars for USA
Proper worldwide launch of pure Turbo cars, three-door at first in black metallic and crimson, 'Inca' alloy wheels, air dams, luxury seat trim, spoilers, factory sunroof
Range includes 99L, GL-EMS, GLE-Turbo (dechromed) two-, three- and five-door options across most of range. GLE trim on five-door shell only
Finnish special for Finland only – stretched 99 four-door and 99 petrol with alternative fuel systems (petrol or paraffin) and plastic fuel tank

Model year 1979
Reduced range in order not to clash with newly launched 900. Extra 99s for UK market due to late RHD 900 production
Changes to rear axle. Modified front suspension. Larger wheel hubs. Interior trim changes. Carry-over of 900 extended bumpers.
99 Turbo with two-door shell. Two-door Turbo in limited numbers. 110bhp engine offered in basic 99 manual cars

Model year 1980
Last 99 made at Trollhättan. All 99s built in Finland from 1980 onwards, at Saab-Valmet Uusikaupunki
99 range rationalized, only GL and Turbo. 900 upgrades carried over to 99 – trim, bumpers, badge style. GLi – rare variant for North America only

Model year 1981
Single model range. 900 carry-over parts and trim. New axle from 900. New steering wheel. H-series engine

Model year 1982
Revised H-series engine. New steel wheels, plus optional alloys

Model year 1983
New 900 style, wide-look grille, trim and chrome changes. Centre console. Five gears. Asbestos-free brakes. Black trim to B pillars. Range slimmed down, carburettor cars returned to line-up in Scandinavia

Model year 1984
Changes to steering-wheel rake and to seats. Low-friction tyre option in Europe. Ignition system changes. 900-style factory sunroof with lip
Last of the line 99, Finnish-built with extra trim and fittings

Model year 1985
End of 99 production in late 1994 after a total of 590,000 cars built

Early British cars did not have opening rear side windows and also came with seatbelts with no tongue or bayonet point; the belt was simply fed into a locking 'klippan' bar-type mechanism.

It was the 99 that brought into being a hallmark Saab feature – the centre-tunnel mounted ignition with reverse gear lock. Siting the ignition key down between the seats reduced the risk of the terrible knee injuries that dashboard-mounted keys inflicted on many unbelted drivers. It also allowed a tie-in with the gearbox. To avoid jamming through icing, the handbrake did not need to be used in the coldest conditions.

Exterior

With their delicate chrome grille, chrome bumpers, chrome window trims and chrome wheel-arch trims, the early cars were shiny, to say the least. The wheel-arch trims were soon deleted. The initial two-door shells had the radio aerial mounting drilled through the scuttle and mounted vertically on the windscreen pillar – a neat solution. The small, chromed rear-view mirrors were mounted at the front base corner of each front side window. (In the original press kit photos, the launch cars had just one rear-view exterior mirror, mounted on the front wing – true old-fashioned style and an indication of a very early-build car. Tester feedback revealed that a wing-mounted mirror was not ideal.)

The original bumper was very low, clearly revealing the sculpted front wing-to-front-undertray join line and giving space below the grille and lamps. Bold and modernistic rectangular badges adorned the flanks of each edge of the bonnet; the black SAAB 99 logo etched into them stayed around right into the 1970s. Early cars also carried the earlier Saab logo, depicting a head-on aircraft silhouette.

One of the 99's oddities was the transverse mounting of the spare wheel, which lay at an angle at the lip of the boot; owners soon got used to it. Another usual feature of the first design specification was a carry-over from the 92-96 series – the freewheel device. This favourite Swedish economy gadget, cable-operated from a switch found down near the footwell, allowed the transmission literally to freewheel. The rest of Europe was less keen on the idea, and this little piece of Swedish eccentricity was quietly disposed of two years later.

The 99 also featured a sliding clamshell bonnet and large wheels.

During the life of the 99, the road-wheel design was changed seven times. All 15in, the first wheels were 4.5in rims, with round holes; in 1972, slots replaced the holes and by 1976, the rim width was 5in. In 1979, star-shaped or triangular-holed wheels were introduced, and in 1982 the holes were changed to rectangular. Latterly, 5.5in rims came in.

1970–72: A CHANGE IN STYLE

By mid-1970 – after only two years on the market – Saab had enlarged the 99's engine to 1854cc, badging the new cars '1.85'. The enlarged engine was offered on the new four-door body shell, which came out in the 1970 model year. The larger-capacity engine needed more cooling air under the bonnet, so the early four-door cars came with two extra air vents – 'nostril'-type below the main grille and above the original bumper.

At first, the larger engine came with fuel injection in the two-door auto only, but it was later made available in carburettor form for both the two- and four-door manual versions. However, when the motoring press tested the 1971 model

By February 1970, Saab had produced half a million cars – the 500,000th was a 99.

By the 1972 model year, Saab had launched the four-door version of the 99 and added revised bumpers and frontal styling.

The revised, moulded-plastic impact-absorbing dashboard of late 1971, which stayed with the car until 1987.

year 99, which appeared late in 1970, it was as the four-door 99E auto with Borg Warner autobox and Bosch fuel injection. The 99 was therefore available with 80bhp, 87bhp and 95bhp engines in a rather confusing mix and match. It was about this time when the freewheel device was quietly dropped.

The only other notable change at this time was the alteration to the exterior rear-view mirrors, which were changed from round to square.

From February 1971 and October 1971 respectively, the four-door onwards, the 99 was given the technical designation of CM4/CM2 series. The numbers were relevant to the body style.

Headlamp wipers were added in late 1971 and a new dashboard was introduced. It had deeply cowled instrument dials, rotary heater controls and a deeper fascia across the car, a larger glovebox and a rather contentious strip of fake wood running across its entire lower edge, highlighted with a 'Fasten Seatbelt' lamp. The new dash design updated

the 99 to a much more modern look; it was clean and timeless, and lasted for a decade.

Bjorn Envall had also performed major surgery on the front of the car, adding deformable, self-repairing, honeycomb-structure rubber bumpers, which were mounted higher than the original chrome bumpers. The new bumpers were unique to Saab. Constructed of cellular-type design, they could compress on impact – at up to 5mph – and then regain their shape. It was a fine answer to a question posed by US car legislation rules in 1972. Other makers simply slapped on angle iron and rubber fences to create so-called 'impact' bumpers, but the Saab solution was much cleverer and neater.

Higher-mounted, bolder side indicator lights represented another move with the times. They changed the frontal aspect of Sason's styling into a more aggressive look.

In mid-1971, a few cars were produced with the revised dashboard, and the original chrome bumpers, but very few of the early four-door cars with the original dashboard have survived from the 1970 model year.

By the end of 1972, the 1.7-litre cars were being phased out and cars featuring the revised Swedish-built 1985cc engine began to come in. Half-way through 1972, Saab launched the EMS (Electronic Manual Special) two-door model, with the new engine, giving the company a sporty, luxury-trimmed car. Through-the-gear acceleration times improved, with 0 to 60mph coming up in under 12 seconds; a top speed of 105mph answered the detractors who felt that the original 99 was too slow. The EMS came with a very unusual alloy wheel design, special seat trim and a black-trimmed grille; a gold bar was added for the US market. Early cars were in metallic Silver Mink, later ones in

Silver Sterling, and later British cars got a black vinyl roof as standard. For the first time on the 99, head restraints were fitted as standard on the EMS. The car also had a tachometer. From 1978, it was offered in some markets with three doors.

FROM 1973

With its new bumpers, revised dashboard, and changed engine, the 99 had established itself successfully as a marque. Changes between 1973 and 1975 were mainly trim- and marketing-related, but Saab continued to tinker with the engineering.

The 1973 model year saw the launch of the new 2-litre Saab revised engine, in the sporty 99 EMS model. A publicity shot shows the special alloy wheel design, square mirror, new grille and various other attractions.

British-spec 99 EMS owned by Colin Townsend Green, circa 1974, with minilite-type wheels.

This profile view of an early model Saab 99 exemplifies a concave rear boot-line, a feature later copied by other manufacturers.

In 1974, Saab launched Envall's three-door Combi Coupe or 'Wagon Back' car. The US version had rare wheel trims

The 1974 plain base model three-door 99 shell in European-spec trim. The 15in wheels fill the arches on high-profile tyres. 'Combi Coupe' script is visible on the rear extractor vent moulding.

The dechromed 99 X7 model, with black window frames, was based on the two-door shell, with the 88bhp engine and manual gearbox only. Some very rare early examples of this car had a new chrome bumper edged in thick black rubber. This 'economy' version of the bumper was almost immediately changed to the thicker, box-section, strut-mounted, all-black rubber self-repairing type.

In 1973–74, US sales of the EMS were going well and the rest of Europe liked the car too. Side-impact doorbars were fitted across the 99 range and the elegant EMS two-door became very popular. Halogen headlamps, revised steering gear and altered front springs all appeared. At this time the first cars from the Belgian factory at Malines, appeared, notching up 5,867 body shells amid 41,124 in Sweden and 15,646 in Finland – serious production numbers at last.

In 1974, Bjorn Envall designed the long-tailed 99 three-door Combi ('Wagon Back' in the USA). Months later, the five-door version, with its C pillar 'opera' side windows, appeared. Both cars had an extended hatchback with an anti-twist design – vertical and span wise shear web fin support structure underneath C pillars to support the low-level opening. By this time, all front seats had been revised and the new versions had high-backed integral headrests. Many of the USA-

The Combi had the feel of a mini-estate car; this shows the rear cabin, with the rear seat still up; note the low sill lip.

Specials

Sweden:	99 four-door auto taxi specification, 1972
Sweden/Finland:	police specification 99 two- and four-door, 1971
Norway:	four-door 99 base model, 1978
Finland:	kerosene-powered version of two-door 99, 1981, Finlandia – long wheelbase 99 in low production numbers
Sweden:	99 X7 base model, 1973
Sweden:	three-door Combi body shell delivery van, 1975
Sweden: UK:	100 99 EMS-Turbo pre-production cars; special chassis nos 900-999 rare, non-listed five-door Turbo models, 25 imported, 1979
UK:	400 extra Turbo models to UK, first UK sales of two-door shell
UK:	99 SAH-tuned special performance kit for 99: Weber carbs, Koni dampers, cosmic 51/2 J wheels, extra gauge on fascia, oil filler and breather pipe modifications
Denmark:	99 Combi three-door van for Danish market only, 1975
Sweden:	four-speed box on base two-door 99, 1984
Sweden/UK:	Ronnie Peterson special build car, three-door with autobox, 2-litre injection engine, air con and special handling kit, side stripes. Supplied by Saab UK
Australia:	99 EMS in three-door version
USA:	99 EMS in two- and three-door styles, three-door known as 'Wagon Back'
USA:	1974 model year 99 LE model. Two-door US model with fuel injection and rare special USA-only wheel trim design (not to be confused with UK spec LEA model)

bound GLE-badged cars were given power steering. This was a real plus for the 99, whose heaviness around town had always been criticized by the British motoring press.

This was also the period of the orange cars, many of which were three-door Combi Coupes. Orange was a popular colour in the 1970s, but it hardly did the Saab any favours in styling terms.

Saab was continuously tweaking its grill designs and another variant on the cross bars and centre box design of the Saab grille motif appeared for 1975. The base model X7 died, to be re-born as a simple 99, with the 2-litre engine. A revised braking system went in across the range. The brakes were changed from ATE to Girling and caliper changes were

The Swedish Police ran a fleet of tuned four-door 99s in the 1970s. This is a 1977 model with enlarged front indicator units.

The 99 GLE – the luxury trimmed car of the late 1970s.

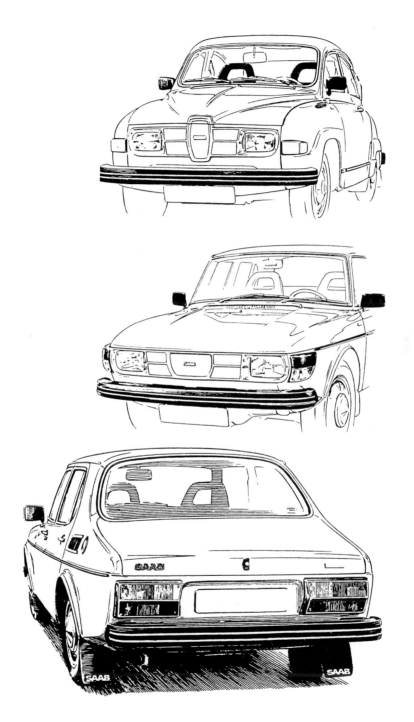

Revised rear lamps on the 99 and a double chrome strip trim on the impact absorbing bumpers arrived for 1977 – the 96 received the 'family look' grille and bumpers too.

made front and rear. A rare three-door 99 van shell appeared, with steel blanking over the rear side windows.

In 1975, the [225bhp] 99 rally car, driven by Stig Blomqvist and co-driver Hans Sylvan, won first time out in the Belgian Boucles de Spa. HRH Prince Bertil, a Saab driver since the 1950s, ordered a four-door 99 GLE, continuing the Swedish Royal family's association with Saab.

For the 1975 model year, there was much that was new. The GLE models arrived with luxury velour trim, all-round headrests, alloy wheels, gold trim highlights, metallic paint and electric mirrors. It looked particularly smart in

metallic copper coral with crimson interior. Chrome wheel-arch finishers made a comeback too. Many GLEs were automatics, and sadly, the later ones seemed to rust more than other 99s.

FINAL YEARS

During the run-out years of the 99, Saab engaged in a series of trim and specification changes, but there was little major structural or engineering progress. Saab kept the car competitive in its sector and continued to focus its attention on its home market, producing special specification cars for Sweden only.

1978: the three-door launch Turbo car in black with 'Inca' wheels.

The model range was first widened and then, with the debut of the 900, rationalized. Alongside this basic ageing process, the Turbo model re-launched the car and the Saab brand on the world market (see page 76). As the Turbo models took over the image of the 99, Saab revamped the basic cars, tweaking the upholstery, the steering wheel and steering geometry, suspension and damping, gearing and drive ratios, and upgrading the instruments and electrics. One of the small changes involved the headlamp wipers, which were altered from a horizontal sweep to a vertical sweep, with the wipers parking at the top of the lens. The modifications kept the car in the running in an increasingly competitive market sector, but in terms of fuel economy the 99 remained firmly in the past (apart from the kerosene-powered special for the Finnish market!).

With four- and then five-door GLE models topping the range, and workhorse L models underlining it, the Saab 99 carved itself a niche in the world market. In the late 1970s, the Saab brand image developed well; the cars were no longer smoky two-strokes, but solid, safe, yet stylistically individual models that were a cut above the norm. Throughout the 1970s, an array of colours was available, with metallic silvers, blues, dark greens, maroons and gunmetal, and a range of solid colours too (although the off-whites, pale greens, and beige-yellows on the colour chart of the mid-1970s were not popular with everyone). Generally, metallics and new colours were first available on the EMS cars, and early EMS cars also had special Silver Mink and Sterling Silver shades. The other 99s of 1970–75 shared colours with the 94-96 range, but the 99 GLE models later received their share of luxury paints and trims.

In Britain, Europe and the USA, the 99 EMS laid the foundations for Saab's more sporting, more capable reputation. It also sold well in Australia. Meanwhile, the 99 soldiered on in reduced variants alongside the new 900, into the early 1980s. The last cars were built in Finland from high-quality steel, with very high standards of paint and sealing, and many can still be found in excellent condition. The last 99 sold in Great Britain was delivered on 16 March 1985.

SPECIALS AND DIFFERENCES

Stretched Models

In the 1980s, the Saab-Valmet plant in Finland produced long-wheelbase 900 CD limousines, but the first special-bodied to car from Saab Finland was actually a stretched four-door 99 saloon, constructed for use by the country's President and higher-ranking ministers.

In 1976, an extra-long stretched 99 was built by Saab for King Carl Gustav XVI of Sweden to use on an official tour of the USA. The little-known 99 Royal Carriage (see the picture on page 70), labelled by Saab as the 'Long Base', featured a massive stretch behind the B pillar. New stretched rear doors had square trailing edges and behind that, the car had the full rear side window of the two-door model. The car had EMS trim detailing and a luxury rear seat and was also equipped with air conditioning.

A Saab 99 Estate

As early as 1964, Sixten Sason had thought of a Saab 99 estate car. His early rendering (see the picture on page 70) shows a sort of coupe-estate in the mould of the later

The 99 Royal Limousine of 1976, with its extended centre portion and rear end of the two-door model.

Rare sketch of the three-door 99 estate that Sixten Sason proposed as early as 1964. Given the right engine and trim, it could have been an early sports estate.

Scimitar and Lancia Beta HPE. It was a three-door with a long rear side panel and very pretty rear end. Sadly, it was not part of the original 99 model line-up – perhaps a rare mistake on the part of Saab!

As late as 1974, there was still talk of the Saab 99 estate. In 1973–74, the project was on, then off for months, with much speculation in the motoring press based on leaked information. The Saab UK Owners Club even published a sketch of the estate car on its magazine's front cover. Word was that the car – codenamed X14 – was a five-door with stylish lines based on the 2-litre 99. It never materialized, however, and Saab missed out on the estate car boom of the late 1970s and early 1980s.

USA, Africa, UK, Netherlands

Main differences for the US market related to engine specifications. Usually, the Americans were offered the larger engine with fuel injection, but with a slightly lower bhp rating because of emissions. Special badges, grilles and trims were used, notably in the EMS version, and all Saab 99s for the USA had to have their glazed-in square head-lamps changed over to four round head-lamps. Side repeater flashers were positioned on the corner of each front and rear wing.

Air conditioning and power steering were available on left-hand drive 99s, notably for cars going to hotter states of

A late 99 two-door model. Note the 'star'-design wheels, which were also seen on the 900.

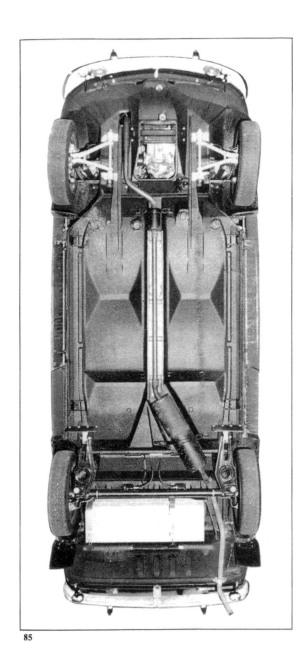

85

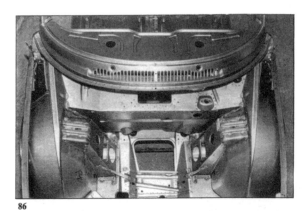

86

87

88

Details of the 99. Left: the flat underfloor; right, from top to bottom: structural details.

1977 – the revised 99. Larger rear lamps, new wheels and trim.

the USA and to the Middle East, where naturally it was most needed.

A number of Saab 99s were exported to Africa by private individuals and a few have been seen in Kenya, Zimbabwe and South Africa.

For the UK, Saab produced a 1984–99 model with two-tone paint in silver over grey with lower panel, with a body kit with boot lid spoiler, A pillar airflow vanes, front and rear under-bumper trays, curved side skirts and cladding, similar to the later Airflow design on the 900. It was a very rare 99 special and virtually unknown outside the Saab cognescenti.

In 1990, a one-off Dutch-registered 99, with the rare 99 body kit in Airflow style, had a 900 T 16-valve engine shoehorned under its bonnet.

99 BECOMES 90

In the early 1980s, Saab found itself without a cheap basic car for its traditional core buyer. The 92-96 had been spot on, as had the 99-900, but the basic models had been overtaken by the upmarket versions and the sporting 900 Turbos. Saab needed something to satisfy its base model buyers – those people who had bought 94-96s and early 99s. The short-term answer was the 90.

Saab created the 90 by mating the front half of the 99 to the rear end of the new two-door 900 booted saloon shell, in 'long-body' 99 style. The result was a strange yet competent car that, despite its rather odd proportions, sold quite well. The original 99 front end – back as far as the B pillars – was given greater cabin space and a

The 99 becomes the 90, with the rear half of the new 900 grafted on.
An unusual combination, but a good car.

Per Ekstrom's self-built 99 street-style special, with lowered roof and 900 Turbo front end.

larger boot, and, along with the mix-and-match body, came a revised engine, larger fuel tank, and suspension changes. A host of 900 model trim items included wider 175/70 low rolling resistance tyres on 15in wheels. Hardened engine valves allowed for unleaded operation, the gearbox was revised and the 100bhp engine – with all its old-style torque – was installed. The 90 used the 99's fascia, which had been around since 1971, complete with its unattractive and fake stick-on wood trim. Sadly, there was no power steering.

For all its unpromising genealogy, the 90 found favour with many drivers, and with road-test reporters – 'old but good' was the general verdict. The 90 was axed after just under three years of production; between the 1985 and 1987 model years, just over 25,000 examples had been sold in Europe, particularly in Scandinavia, the Netherlands, the UK and Germany. Today, surprisingly few 90s remain on British roads, but many Dutch owners are still driving theirs, which have remained smart and rust-free.

6   Turbo Years

The science of turbocharging was not new for the Swedes. Saab had years of experience in turbocharging and in supercharging, first in working on the diesel engines of Scania, the company with which it merged, and second in its involvement in the aviation industry. Its technical knowledge in the fields was extensive. Swedish engineers were also familiar with the device of using highly efficient impellor wheels with blades or vanes, as in the workings of a turbocharger. The hydroelectric power plants of Trollhättan had used such devices for years to capitalize on the natural resource of hydrodynamic flow. Adapting the essence of that formula to air-driven turbo impellors was not far removed from the company's experience.

Early publicity shot featuring a Saab Viggen fighter pilot and Stig Blomqvist.

BACKGROUND

Saab believed in marrying economy with effectiveness of design, form with function. In the mid-1970s, however, the engineers realized that they had an engine problem. Performance, economy and concerns about emissions were all coming to the fore – particularly in the USA, which was a market that Saab could not afford to ignore. Saab's way of thinking would not allow them simply to create a big-bore torque-laden engine for the 99 and the 900; Saab engineers preferred to find another way around the issue.

In solving the problem, Saab turned the alternative world of turbocharging on its head. Turbocharging experts at Porsche and BMW had always bolted on their turbo blowers, to increase the maximum power at top-end maximum revs. It was ideal for storming down the Mulsanne straight at Le Mans or around the Nürburgring. The surge and wail at top speed was what compressed-injection turbocharging had been all about. Saab realized that, for its cars and in its markets, it was not top speed that counted. More important was mid-range torque – that vital period between 50 and 70mph when a driver pulls out to overtake. Saab's aim in turbocharging was to keep the driver out of danger as much as possible; the power boost should enhance safety, not detract from it.

Mellde and Gillbrand had worked for years on engines for Saab, revitalizing the old Triumph engine, and pushing for the Ford-derived V4 unit that transformed the 96 series cars. They were joined by a new name – Bengt Gadefelt – who had been one of the top diesel men at Scania, refining the turbocharging concept for Saab-Scania trucks. The highly experienced Josef Eklund was another member of the development team.

Per Gillbrand, contributor to the Saab Turbo legend.

Also involved was Englishman Geoffrey Kershaw, ex-Rolls-Royce apprentice and later head of Turbo-Technics Ltd. Kershaw was brought in as early as 1974 via Saab's links with Scania's turbocharged trucks. Scania had worked with Garret (AiResearch). He spent many months with Saab and ended up driving home in one of the 99 EMS development cars.

Gillbrand, Eklund, Pettersen and Gadefelt lobbied management for the financial resources to allow them to develop the turbo option, and steered them away from the idea of building a V8 powerplant. The links with Scania would prove useful and, by 1975, Saab was able to announce that it was 'going turbo' (keeping quiet about the fact that it had already turbocharged a 96 rallycross car in 1974!). This team of engineers took the concept of the basic blower turbocharger and redefined it for the Saab task.

THE WASTE–GATE THEORY

The turbocharger had been used in truck and marine engines for over a decade, seen as a way of blowing vast amounts of extra power into an engine up to maximum revs. The idea was that the extra stresses and heat involved would be contained – or not, in which case, the engine would blow – depending on the application. Robustly constructed truck engines could easily contain the forces of turbocharging, but car engines were less resilient.

This basic type of turbocharging gave huge gains in horsepower, but in a way that was unacceptable for everyday driving. Revs and exhaust gasses would build, the heavily built turbo wheel would spin up, and then after a time delay – known as 'lag', the turbo would cut in and fire away. It was great for a racing car, a boat or a heavy truck, but not for a road-going saloon.

In studying the turbocharger concept, Gadefelt and the team remembered that, in the Second World War, the Americans had added turbochargers to their aircraft engines to provide boost at high altitude. The turbos had been geared to perform when needed. The Americans had also developed a turbo for airline engine use, which came in like a clutch when demanded. In its trucks, with their slogging diesel engines, Scania had developed turbos – with a lag built into them.

Saab wanted to find out how to gear the turbo concept, yet make it simpler and more durable. There had to be a way of

Stan Wennlo, who gave the go-ahead for the Turbo after a late-night test drive of a 99 development car. Legend has it that he reported back to the team from a public telephone outside a café.

detuning the turbocharger, making it only work as a turbo when demanded by the driver's right foot. Further refinements came from making the turbine wheel less heavy and easier-spinning, so that it 'picked up' at lower revs, reducing lag. The turbo unit was smaller and lighter and had a totally different modus operandi.

Blow valves had been used in exhaust systems to detune turbos, but the Saab team was the first to come up with the waste-gated turbo – an 'on-demand blow' – and then the light-pressure turbo. The concept was based on aviation engineering – in simple terms, it used a bypass theory pressure relief valve, like a jet engine but without an afterburner! The turbo in the exhaust system only operated when sufficient demand was made, and as soon as the boost has been delivered, it was constrained by deliberately spilling, or wasting off, the charge. The tuned system would shut out the turbo unit and the car would become normally aspirated once again. At high revs, the waste-gate spilt excess exhaust air away from the turbo – preventing it from running away with itself.

It was simple but it was a superb way of tuning the turbo for everyday road use. Later on its development, using spare air in the exhaust, the turbo could be kept spinning at 'standby' low revs. With its vanes aerodynamically tuned, the turbo could be made to take on a whole new character.

Saab's turbo concept first opened the door to practical turbocharger use in mass production. Today, the light-pressure turbo with waste-gate is used across the entire motor industry.

CONCEPT AND DETAILS

Garret AiResearch, a US turbo-making company that had already worked with Porsche, became the manufacturer of the Saab turbo unit. Before its production, the inlet air drive had been state of the art; Saab's development of the exhaust back pressure actuation was to make turbo use acceptable in an everyday car.

Experiments with early full-bore turbo settings were conducted on EMS models; half a dozen 99s were equipped in late 1976. The members of the engine design team were convinced that they had found something special, and top management were soon persuaded once they had driven the experimental cars.

Efficiency and Performance

Improving the efficiency of the existing engine had become vital because of stringent new US legislation on emissions, particularly in the state of California. American manufacturers responded in a rather contradictory manner, by simply upping the cc level, then detoxing their cars' emissions with power-sapping, gas-guzzling devices. Saab's Turbo cars for California came with fuel injection and Lambda-type oxygen sensors fitted in the manifold, to monitor the air mix discharge. By sending a series of electronic pulses to a sensor, the Lambda unit 'thought' for itself and automatically changed settings in the injection system. This system, allied to a small catalyst, satisfied California's 1977 requirements on emissions. And with 133bhp, the cars competed well with the European-spec non-catalytic cars, which offered 140bhp at first.

The overall torque and horsepower increases for the Saab Turbos were significant. The torque curves were rather peaky, but as long as the peak was at a lower rev range – where it was needed for mid-range punch – this did not matter. Torque was up 45 per cent and power ratings rose 23 per cent. The torque figure on a good engine equals the bhp figure, but Saab's new engine offered 145bhp and the torque figure shot up to 174lb/ft at 3,500rpm. Moreover, the effect on the mpg rating was minimal; the turbo only cut in for approximately 20 per cent of driving time, so the engine performed well in terms of fuel consumption.

Back in 1972, Saab's clever redefinition of the old Triumph engine contributed to the cars' capacity to achieve huge mileages and to handle the increased pressures of a turbo. They had already given it a stronger crank and a strengthened head. Now, in the mid-1970s, all they had to do was revise the valve seats and stems, using stiffer steel and sodium treatment, incorporate heat-dissipating improvements in the piston design and revise the camshaft. An oil cooler was used and the exhaust was different.

Saab's turbo engine could run with fuel injection. The turbo was mounted near the front of the engine and was clothed with heat shields and piping. The unit had an earthy, rumbling sound. At speed, the turbo vanes revolved at anything up to an average of 50,000 to 80,000rpm and they were, in fact, tested to 200,000rpm. The characteristic turbo 'whistle' was audible at about 60mph onwards. Incidentally, adding the turbocharger had the extra benefit of smoothing out the exhaust note and quietening the engine noise.

The first production turbo unit was so well tuned that a feather-light touch on the throttle could fool it into remaining dormant. However, it was sufficiently tractable that a good shove on the pedal could make it cut in, without having to drop a gear (thereby aiding fuel economy, too). Adding the turbo to the 99 had necessitated a higher final drive ratio, to meet the needs of response and fuel economy.

Saab had got it just right. The motoring press loved the first Saab Turbos.

Potential Problems and Reliability

Saab was of course most concerned about the reliability of the blown engine. The racing Porsches and the BMW 2002 cars both blew turbos and Saab desperately wanted to avoid broken-down turbo cars and warranty claims. As it happened, there were a few problems, but the early production turbo cars kept going well.

The turbo unit began to burble at just over 1,500rpm in any drive gear. By 2,500rpm, boost was building up to produce

a shove, with the turbo unit spinning at 55,000rpm, when the engine revs reached 3,500rpm. Instead of cutting in like a switch, the unit engaged more gradually. There was lag at first, but it was possible to drive around it. The press made much of the lag factor, yet it was minimal compared with other applications and, after a few years of development, it was virtually eliminated.

Owners were advised to let a Turbo model idle for a few minutes before turning the engine off, to allow the turbo unit to cool and the heat to soak away, and so that the area would remain lubricated. Doing this undoubtedly prolonged the life of the unit, which would survive for 50,000 to 70,000 miles before needing to be replaced. Some Saab turbo units *did* blow earlier than this, but the engineers at Saab worked hard to resolve the problems. With their constant improvements, the long-term reliability of a turbo became more of a reality.

THE FIRST TURBO CARS

Launch and Reaction

By late 1976, the Saab engine department was gearing up for the launch of the first Turbo model. In spring 1977, 100 99 Turbo three-door body shells, tagged 'EMS-Turbo', were released into specially chosen hands for a 'field trial'. These early-build prototypes provided Saab with an opportunity to sort out any teething troubles before the full mass-market release of the model for the 1978 model year.

The emphasis may have been on the US emissions legislation, but the performance potential of the new Turbo model was very exciting. By this time, Saab's successful 96 rally cars had been pensioned off and the 99 had taken over at the Saab rally team. The 99 was bigger and heavier, and even a dedicated Saab fanatic could not describe its steering as light or responsive. The job of rallying a 99 was not an easy one, but the team still scored many notable successes. Inevitably, the drivers were keen on taking the turbo unit rallying; in the end, the Saab 99 Turbo Group 4 rally car was boosted to as much as 270bhp.

The production Saab 99 Turbo was launched at the 1977 Frankfurt Motor Show, offered with three doors, painted black with front under-bumper air dam, and a rear-lip, vortex-tuning spoiler halfway down the rear hatchback. The motor-ing press loved it; according to them, Saab's turbo unit had transformed the 99 model range from safe but a bit ponderous to exciting and exotic.

The reporter at *Motor* magazine wrote the following:

> If the maximum speed of nearly 120mph isn't impressive enough, then you need to look no further than the remarkable top-gear acceleration figures to put the turbo in perspective; between 40 and 100mph, the Saab accelerates faster than just about any four-seater saloon in the world. And that means overtaking and cross-country ability of the sort hitherto the preserve of expensive exotica.

Saab 99 Three-Door Turbo (1978 model year)

Engine:

Type:	four-cylinder in line, longitudinal mounting, iron block, alloy head, chain-driven OHC, 8-valve head
Capacity:	1985cc Bosch Jetronic fuel injection; Garrett AiResearch turbocharger
Top speed:	120mph (192km/h)
0–60mph:	9.1 secs
Max power:	145bhp (DIN) at 5,000rpm (108.10Kw)
Boost:	0.09 bar (1.2 bar max rating)
Torque at 3,500rpm:	174lb/ft (233Nm)

Transmission:
Four-speed gearbox; drive to front wheels through driveshafts of unequal length

Suspension:
Wishbones and dampers to front
Coil springs with panhard rod, watts links and twin arms to rear

Tyres:
Pirelli CN36

Body:
Steel unit monocoque with reinforcing beams in roof and pillars
Side-impact beams in doors
Fuel tank ahead of rear axle
Self-repairing bumpers

Dimensions:
Wheelbase 97.5in (2.48m)
Length 178.3in (4.53m)
Width 66in (1.68m)

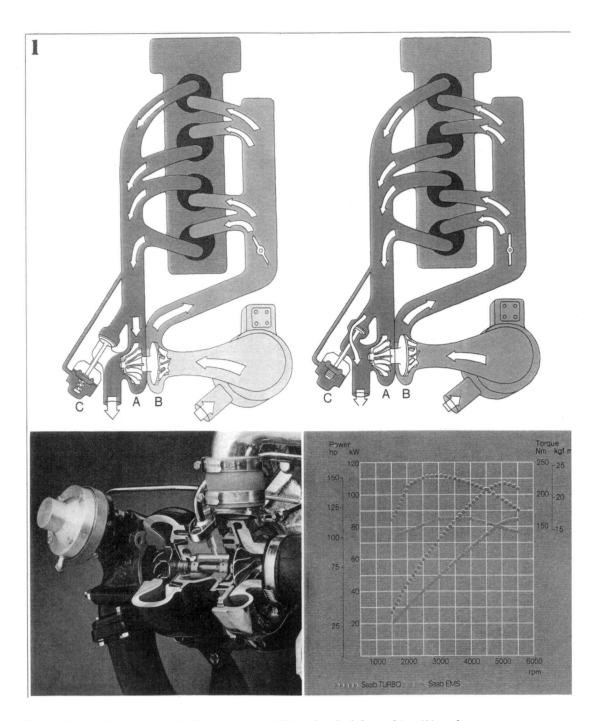

The workings of the turbo unit. The waste gate (C) is ahead of the turbine (A) and impellor (B). Closing the gate 'charges' the system.

The 99 Turbo was immediately popular in the USA, where it could zoom past the larger V8-powered American cars. The Germans loved the car's *autobahn*-storming potential and the British found the Turbo superb in their country, where swift, safe overtaking was crucial. Their roads – which required the driver to see a gap, check the mirrors and floor the accelerator pedal – revealed the turbo lag to a greater degree than roads elsewhere in Europe or in the USA. Driving on a trailing throttle, with the engine 'off the cam', meant that the turbo needed time to spool up for overtaking and that meant that there was little boost available for instant overtaking on twisting, slower roads, or coming off roundabouts. British drivers had to learn to tailor their turbo technique. It did not stop them buying the 99 Turbo, even though its price – £7,850 – was relatively high at the time for a four-cylinder car. Saab was clearly pitching it at the quality end of the market.

View of the turbo engine unit 1983, with its 45-degree angled head and turbo pipework.

Two- and three-door 99 Turbos of 1981.

Front suspension, with double wishbone set-up.

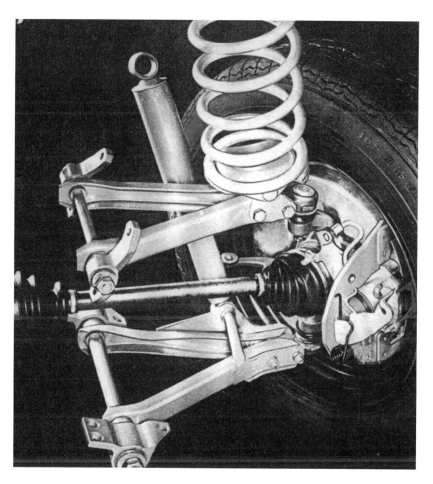

The Saab 99 Turbo became an instant classic. It was *the* performance car of the late 1970s, representing a unique moment in motoring history, and appealing to a wide range of buyers, from the 'ordinary' driver to the serious sports-car enthusiast.

Features and Specials

The 1978–81 Turbos came with unique 'Inca' alloy wheels. The design was based on a South American architectural motif – a stepped, pyramid design emanating from a square-shaped hub. The wheels were never copied, and are now highly desirable. Some of the US- and Australian-spec cars came with Ronal 'minilite' tubular-spoked wheels of rally-type design.

Saab's special badge for the Turbo featured an 'o' at the end shaped like a turbo wheel.

The interior of the Turbo had a centre console, a special three-spoke steering wheel with a large triangular padded boss, and seats trimmed in velour with a diagonal pleat motif. A boost gauge was at first mounted on the windscreen pillar and then moved to a high spot on the fascia top, close to the driver's line of sight. It indicated when the boost began to build, and then when it had exhausted itself via the waste-gate control sensors.

The exterior of the Turbo featured chrome trim on the window surrounds and bumpers; this slightly dated look was soon changed, with a black anodized finish on the 900.

In 1979, a rare batch of 25 five-door 99 Turbo models was produced. Several were finished in very smart metallic crimson. Their existence is often denied, but at least two were sold by Scottish Saab aficionado and dealer Alistair Robertson, of St Claire Motors.

Late in 1980, an 'extra' batch of 99s was released on to the UK market, after the original three-door Turbo 99 had been withdrawn to make way for the 900 Turbo. Loosely based on the original rally 'homologation' production run, the two-door car was available in red or black, and benefited from many of the 900 specification upgrades, notably the suspension improvements. It was lighter than the hatchback original, and faster, knocking over a second off the 0–60mph sprint time, to achieve 8.00. The 60–80mph times were also shorter, providing even more overtaking performance. The interior was identical to that of the original Turbo. It is unclear how many of the 'extra' cars were sold, but reports vary between 400 and 800.

With the 99 Turbo, Saab had started a revolution. Soon after, every car manufacturer – even the Japanese – turned to turbocharging.

DEVELOPMENTS: 99 AND 900 TURBOS

One of the world's 10 best cars for the 80s. (US magazine *Road and Track* on the Saab 900 Turbo)

Water Injection

One of the early developments was a water-injection system that blended cooling water with a small percentage of methanol and injected it into the inlet air charge via a pump. This was not a 'full-time' device, and the water was injected only when the boost pressure reached 0.8 bar. The water in the airstream cooled down the air and increased its density, giving a bigger 'charge' and creating up to 40 extra bhp. Thus the engine was fooled into thinking that it had an even higher compression ratio than before. The water reserves had to be monitored. If the water-cooling system ran out, a seized turbo unit would result.

In 1982, Saab produced a 'sport kit' for the 99 Turbo and early model 900 Turbos, which upped the boost and added 30bhp.

Intercooler

The water-injection system was short-lived. Saab's longer-term solution was the intercooler. The charge air was threaded through an intercooler water-cooling jacket, entered the turbo cycle at a lower operating temperature and thus cooled the turbo itself. There was not enough room under the bonnet of the 99 for a full-bore intercooler, so it was the 900 that really benefited from the intercooler theory. Some Saab enthusiasts did plumb in a smaller intercooler unit to their 9, but it was rarely a success.

Later Modifications

In later years, the 900 Turbo series gained a 16-valve head, the intercooler, fuel injection, automatic performance control (see page 87) and direct ignition. In 1985, the Saab 16-valve turbo engine became the world's first turbocharged 16-valve head design in series production. The cars were designated 900 T16 and put out 175bhp, achieving a 135mph (216km/h) top speed and 0 to 60mph in 7 seconds.

Saab 900 Turbo 16 (1984)	
Engine	
Type:	four cylinders, 16-valve APC control. Garrett AiResearch T3 model turbocharger with intercooler. Waste-gate control Increased airflow cooling in engine bay
Max power:	175bhp (130Kw) at 5,000rpm
	Bosch electronic injection
Note:	202lb/ft torque (274Nm) at 3,200rpm

In 1981, the 900's second year of existence, Saab made a significant change to the turbo unit. Prior to this date, the 99 and 900 Turbos had used 'poppet' valve turbo waste-gate actuation. In 1981, Saab brought in a new type of waste-gate that had an integrated, swing-type mechanism The turbine was also smaller, giving better response at low rpm.

Saab also addressed the aerodynamics inside the turbocharger as it developed the concept. On the 99 Turbo, a surge of air mass was taken back into the turbo after the waste-gate had cut out (when the driver lifted off the pedal), causing a bubble of extra reverse airflow to block the system – just like a compressor stall in a jet turbine engine. This caused the turbo wheel to stall and allowed it to spool down, causing lag. In extreme cases, particularly where the turbo output supply and pressure rating had been tweaked, the differences in air masses could actually break the turbo's turbine wheel. Saab worked on easing off the strength of the air charge and towards tuning the turbine. The result was the seamless, if ultimately less powerful light-pressure turbo.

Saab tried another solution to the problem, which involved fitting a 'dump valve' into the turbo system, allowing the excess intake air to bleed off. After-market dump-valve systems dispensed with the traditional dump-valve design, which used a diaphragm, and used a moulded airflow valve set-up instead. One notable system was supplied by British tuner Trent Saab of Nottingham for the 900 Turbo (especially the T16 models).

AUTOMATIC PERFORMANCE CONTROL ('APC') SYSTEM

Less than three years into the life of the Saab Turbo, and as the worldwide sales success of the 900 Turbo models began, Saab introduced another major development in the design and use of turbocharging. This, the automatic performance control system, was badged as 'APC' on the rear of the cars.

APC was based on a simple yet incredibly effective theory. It was the first device that enabled a turbo engine to 'think' for itself, constantly tailoring previously set values to the state of the engine and the type and grade of fuel used. In effect, it monitored the cylinder head for fuel pre-detonations – or 'knock' – and then adjusted the settings accordingly to deal with them. The engine became far more efficient, particularly with the new 16-valve head, which had been grafted on to the 8-valve head spec. This major step forward, an early style of 'lean burn', was rewarded with industry prizes and press acclaim.

APC was also tied up with the 16-valve head – another Saab 'first'. The first Saab 4-valves-per-cylinder 2-litre engine – the first Saab 16-valve unit – was actually made in 1976 and fitted to the first versions of the 99 EMS rally car. This car boasted 200bhp, due to major cylinder head improvements, and an 11.7:1 compression ratio.

Pre-detonation of fuel within the combustion chamber is linked to the octane quality of the fuel – and to the charge of fuel-air mix in which it operates, which is affected by the turbo installation. Saab recognized the possibility of tuning the level of boost as a corollary to the level of pre-detonation, caused by octane variations, in order to create a far more fuel-efficient engine cycle. The problem lies in how to gauge accurately the charge or mix in the cylinder head prior to the spark phase and subsequent combustion. With compression ratio, temperature, humidity, pressure, and so on, all taken into account, the parameters of ignition, detonation and turbocharging need to be mobile. The graph of these effects is not stable and the engine suffers because it cannot tune itself.

The APC system relies on three main sensors connected to electronic measuring gear: a pressure recording device in the intake phase; a detonation sensor mounted within the cylinder head; and a sensor in the electrical system (distributor) that charts ignition timing via rpm. The three sensor signals are relayed to a central 'brain', which computes the information to relay a signal to the waste-gate set-up of the turbo unit. A solenoid connecting the exit phase of the charge with the pressure readings at the inlet side of the charge allows the differences to be signalled. The whole system, in other words, is based on a detonation sensor that automatically adapts to perceived changes, offering variable boost set by the engine itself.

The waste-gate setting of 3.7psi – the point at which it bypasses the system – becomes relevant because that is the rate at which the system operates in moderate boost. However, when the signals inform of a change in detonation parameters, the waste-gate is programmed to stay closed for longer, delaying the bypass bleed off, raising the boost level and creating a change in compression figures and parameters. By concentrating on the 'knock' or detonation cycle, the engine can also figure out how far the accelerator has been pressed down and incorporate ambient temperature, barometric pressure, operating altitude, humidity and a whole host of previously set parameters. Incredibly, all these complicated signals are computed up to 9 times per second.

Saab's APC system avoided the need for fiddling with the ignition cycle timing in the combustion phase, preventing starvation, alternate oversupply, and temperature rises in the cylinder head. It allowed changes in the combustion cycle without affecting fuel economy and was, of course, tailored to the turbocharger of which it was a part. Adding valves to the cylinder head – as Saab did to turn the 8-valve turbo into a 16-valve turbo – posed few problems and aided piston, combustion/swirl and efficiency.

Today, most turbochargers on mass-market cars are of the light-pressure tuned variety, and tend to use dump valves, in a fitting testimony to Saab's pioneering turbo work.

DRIVING IMPRESSIONS – THE 99 TURBO

Before the Turbo, the 99 was a solid and strong, if a touch basic, car. Those early models had integrity and the usual Saab road holding and capable dynamics, notably excellent steering feedback and

1978 Saab 99 'Turbo' branding – the original Turbo brochure cover.

brake feel. Of course the front-wheel drive played a major role in creating the feel of the car.

With the advent of the fuel-injected EMS model, the 99 with a, by now, 1985cc engine, alloy wheels, geometry changes and an altogether more sporting feel, took on a new character. The EMS felt less wooden, a touch sharper, and certainly it was faster. 60mph came up in around 10 seconds – a respectable figure for the era – and the top speed was 110mph (180km/h). Through the gears performance was strong, too: plenty of torque, if not ultimate speed. In fact, although the shared-ancestry engine of the Triumph Dolomite Sprint pushed that car to 60mph in 8 seconds, the 99 EMS figures were on a par with BMWs and Alfa Romeos of the time. Best of all, the Saab did not need constant gear changing, long-legged torque coming into play again.

For the mid-1970s, the 99 EMS carved itself a niche in Britain, Europe and then in America; it was not the quickest car in its class, but it was consistent, reliable and obviously strong, with a hint of sporting character without at any stage appearing brash. Somehow, although the likes of Ford's Cortina 2000E was a competitor, the Saab effect occupied different ground. Yet by the late 1970s even the EMS was beginning to look dated. The styling was still fresh, but the chrome trim, vinyl roof and general feel had become a bit to set in its way. The Saab fanatics still loved the 99 range, of course, but the warning signs were ominous. All was saved by the turbo – itself initially branded as the EMS Turbo – notably in America, before the Turbo brand marketing machine cut in.

Driving a Saab turbo meant that unless you had previous experience, a whole new technique was needed. Around town and on urban roads, the Turbo felt very much like a normal 99: a touch ponderous and feeling as thought the torque band had to be wound up. But by revving beyond 1,800rpm and upping the cross-country speeds, the Turbo would spin up and cut in, whisking the 99 Turbo driver into a whole new world. Show the Turbo a long straight, floor the throttle and ignore the temptation to change down a gear, and after a slight delay the engine and charger would spin away, literally pushing the driver back into the seat as the 99 took flight.

By running in fifth gear at motorway speeds, the revs could be kept at a point where the turbo was just spinning slightly, ready to give an instant response; whereas on cross country roads you had to plan ahead slightly, analyzing forthcoming performance opportunities in order to drop a gear, spool up the turbo and get the boost to coincide with the overtaking manoeuvre – true Turbo driving style. This effect was best used for overtaking manoeuvres on wide A-roads and also cross-country on B-roads – slow-moving traffic could be dismissed with the greatest of ease and, more importantly, safety, as the time spent on the wrong side of the road was minimized by the Turbo's performance in the 30–50mph (50–80km/h) and 50–70mph (80–110km/h) bands.

The 0–60mph time of 8.5 seconds was the stuff of real performance and, providing you kept the turbo on song at around 3,500rpm, spectacular progress could be made. Motorway overtaking saw the 70–90mph (110–145km/h) sector coming up in under 8 seconds – again, real super-car-eating performance. Top speeds of 120mph (190km/h) were possible, but the car had an ignition cut-out at 6,000rpm to preserve the engine.

By making full use of the gearbox, electrifying performance could be called up. Care had to be taken on bends, where too much throttle, or the boost cutting in, could create dangerous torque steer. If you set the car up properly, though, and remembered the Turbo driving technique, the car could be made to storm across country, not just fly along the fast lane of the motorway. The steering was heavy, as with all 99s, but weighted up nicely in bends. Roll angles were low and the ride had plenty of damping and controlled rebound, courtesy of sports dampers.

Driving the 99 Turbo was fun, it gave those who could not afford a Ferrari or a Porsche an insight into true performance driving, and it created a whole new world for a mass market of drivers. Fast, quiet and stable, yet strong and reliable, the 99 Turbo had real character and was an instant performance car icon. Road testers at the time used words like 'relentless', 'spectacular' and 'rocket-ship urge'. The fact was that, despite the hype, the 99 Turbo brought supercar performance to the ordinary motorist, and reliably so as well. This had not been done before by such means.

Driving the 99 Turbo had to be experienced to be believed. Seen from the here and now, that might sound like hype, but in the context of its time Saab, that maker of good but dull cars, according to the motoring press, had achieved a minor miracle in the 99 Turbo.

7 Reincarnation – the 900

By the late 1970s, Saab, although success-ful, was in a quandary. The company was coming close to having only one car in its range – the 99. In 1980, its involvement in the small-car sector was over, with the end of the 96, which had survived longer than anyone might have expected. By late 1984, the 99 would be gone too. The extra Turbo models – over 10,000 of them – helped keep Saab alive, but in 1977 the company had to make a decision on a totally new model. And a new model needed time. Where should they go from there?

Should Saab produce another mass-market workhorse car, or an entirely new upmarket model? Could it afford a totally new car in any sector? A small car was an essential – indeed, the company even sold

One of the early five-door 900s with 'turbine'-style alloy wheels, 'opera' windows, dechroming and long-nose look.

jointly badged Saab-Lancia models in Sweden for a while – but, for a new small car, the designers would have to start from scratch. If the managers made the decision to go upmarket, the 99 might just provide a base, saving time and money and giving the designers some breathing space to plan a completely new model for the late 1980s. New safety legislation in the USA, one of Saab's most important markets, meant that the 99 body shell needed attention anyway.

The result of all the discussions was a compromise, but a good one none the less. The 900, conceived during the management of Sten Wennlo, provided Saab with time and profits, and enable the company to make its move in the late 1980s to the 9000.

THE CONCEPT OF THE 900

The 99 GLE had enjoyed good sales, and Saab believed that a move upmarket would be profitable. At the time, Volvo was also doing well with upmarket cars – the 144 and the 164 – which provided a basis for the later enlarged and modified 200 series. (Incidentally, the idea of a Saab-Volvo merger had come and gone.) Saab determined to move firmly into the sector of the market that was dominated by BMW, Audi and Rover.

Saab hoped to make more money by moving upmarket, but first it had to spend some. The designers took the basic 99 Combi-style five-door body shell and removed its nose, which had begun to look

X-ray view of the 900.

ABOVE: *Early model 900 during final assembly at Trollhättan. Note the inner wing structure, exposed by the absence of the 'clamshell' bonnet. Saab used both the 'production line' and 'group' assembly methods to build the 900 between 1979 and 1993.*

RIGHT: *Safety-cage structure of the 900.*

a touch short-fronted compared with the five-door Combi's long-tail look. They grafted on an extension in front of the front wheels, and added 2in (50mm) to the wheelbase by stretching the car at the scuttle. There were many serious structural implications in doing this, but there were also benefits: a larger crush zone in accidents (satisfying the 30mph impact test demanded by the new US legislation); far more space under the bonnet for re-engineering and engine changes; and better 'offset' crash performance. The engineers would be able to modify and improve the existing range of engines, and there

was even room at last for power steering, to put an end to the 99's heavy steering.

Major changes to trim, suspension, fittings, brakes, and many other detail improvements effectively created a new car for Saab. A completely new interior comprised an attractive ergonomic 'cockpit'-style dashboard and fascia. A unique cabin-air filtering system gave the cleanest cabin air of any car, ever, on a par with the high-efficiency air-particle filters found in 1990s airliners.

The 900's steering and suspension geometry allowed it to carry straight on in the event of a high-speed blow-out on one

of the front wheels. Even at motorway speeds, the Saab-tuned suspension and steering remained stable – a rare quality in any car. Despite having nearly 60 per cent of its empty weight over the front wheels, and a c.g. that moved rearwards when the car was heavily loaded, the front-drive 900 was no lurching understeerer either. Even in Turbo guise it did not suffer any 'lift-off' handling changes or switches. Saab put a lot of work into the handling, and it was well rewarded.

The 900's front coil springs were interesting in that they were pivot-mounted. This allowed the springs to retain their capabilities without being deflected along their longitudinal axis. A steel-mesh bellows device incorporated into the steering column collapsed on impact from either direction, offering excellent shock-absorbing qualities.

LAUNCH AND REVIEWS

Announced in the spring of 1978, the 1979 model year 900 was launched in late 1978. The Americans received their cars soon after the Swedes, but Britain had to wait a bit longer for right-hand drive cars. The market responded well to the car. Despite resembling the old 99 – particularly from the rear – Saab had pulled it off. The 900 was greeted not as a facelift, but as a new model in its own right. Some even thought that its long-bonneted, swept-rear look was 'sexy' – an unusual reaction for a Saab!

Saab publicized the 900 as the 'most intelligent car ever built'. Its thoughtful design features and responsive handling were streets ahead of any of the best American front-drivers of the time. The US motoring press loved it. A reporter at *Motorsports Weekly* wrote the following:

There is certainly no other car in the world I can think of right now that is capable of carrying five adults in comfort while matching the performance, ride and handling and fuel economy balance of the Saab Turbo. It's in a class by itself...the most exciting sports sedan in America.

In the UK, *Autosport* said the following of the 900 Turbo:

It is difficult to put into words the charm and fascination of this remarkable car. As a combination of performance, refinement, and fuel economy, it stands alone, and the integrity of its engineering and the quality of its finish are second to none. If you were conclude from the above that this is just about the best motor car which is at present being made, anywhere, you wouldn't be far wrong.

The 900 was greeted with similar praise in Australia and elsewhere in Europe.

Saab had hit the mark. The 1982 sales figures were as follows: worldwide total 63,400; US total 18,003; British total 7,008.

In 1983, Saab announced that it had built its 100,000th turbocharged car. At that time, Saab was the world's biggest maker of turbocharged cars, although Japanese manufacturer Mitsubishi – which had picked up directly on Saab's achievements – soon took over the title.

NEW CAR, NEW STRUCTURE

If the 99 had been tough, the 900 had to be both tough and more adaptable. Underneath the revised styling – designed by Bjorn Envall – lay a thoroughly revised chassis.

Crash Testing

Aluminium replaced steel in the bumper support beams, and deliberate crush cans worked into the front wheel arches to

ABOVE: The 'Toad', the widened 96 that was used for early secret testing of the 99 floorpan and drivetrain.

LEFT: X7 – the rare base model 99 with chrome bumpers and economy trim, available in Scandinavia for a short period.

BELOW: The first of the five-door body styles; note the 'opera' windows in the C post.

ABOVE: Brochure spread from 1968.

RIGHT: Original 99 launch brochure, September 1968.

BELOW: The 99 EMS looks fresh and futuristic with its compound curves and swept rear angles.

The 1973 US-spec 99 EMS model, with four round headlamps, side stripes and special alloy wheels.

ABOVE: The 1977 launch car in three-door body with black paint and crimson velour interior.

BELOW: 99 wearing a front-spoiler kit and fog lamps, from around 1977.

RIGHT: The two-door 99 Turbo in metallic crimson with 'Inca' wheels – the ultimate Saab Turbo?

LEFT: 99 GL three-door Combi Coupé of 1978, one the most popular 99 variants.

LEFT: The cabin of Ted Jackson's Classic 900, with wood trim and optional Saab sports steering wheel.

BELOW: The 90 model of 1986 – a 99 front and 900 two-door rear creating a simple but effective car, if a touch long-tailed.

900 undergoing crash testing at the Saab safety centre.

ABOVE: 900 in a Japanese setting.
Japan's Saab owners' club has
over 100 members and the Classic
900 has cult status in the country.

ABOVE: The Classic 900 Turbo of
1980, with 'turbine'-style rather
than 'Inca' wheels.

BELOW: This 900 may look basic,
but it neatly captures the essence
of the work of Sason and Envall.

ABOVE: *Original 900 interior.*

ABOVE: *The four-door body emphasizes the Saab style. The 1983 version had a revised grille and extra brightwork.*

BELOW: *The first 900 convertible at the 1983 Frankfurt Motor Show.*

ABOVE: *Super Saab – the
original Turbo 16 Aero of 1984.
Note front spoiler lip, three spoke
alloys and pearlescent painted
body and body kit package. The
rear spoiler was standard size.*

RIGHT: *Chris Day's Haymill-
sponsored car competed in the saloon
car challenge series of the 1980s.*

BELOW: *The Imola Red colour
looked good on the body of the
two-door 900 Turbo. This car
has the later wheels shared
with the 9000 model.*

Later slant-nosed 900, with body kit and 'Super Inca' wheels.

LEFT: *Underbonnet view of the last-of-the-line 900 'Ruby' model. Note the curve of the scuttle, the inner wing structure and the bonnet-locking rails.*

BELOW: *'New' 900 – pure Saab style, surely?*

absorb more crash energy. The 99's slot-like front windscreen was deepened by 1in (75mm) at the lower edge, by incorporating a lower scuttle and removing the air duct, which was replaced by aerodynamically tuned twin inlet and outlet vents in the bonnet. After a couple of years, these were changed to one vent, giving a deeper windscreen. The bonnet was programmed to fold at specific points. At its rear, it was locked down into the structure via a rail and tie system that added vital stiffness at the back of the engine compartment and stopped the bonnet lifting up towards the windscreen. This was a known feature of front-hinged bonnets that became apparent in the early crash tests on the 99 and the 900. The engine was also designed to drop down in a heavy crash, reducing

footwell intrusion – so often a problem on front-drive cars, and especially on transverse-engined ones (although the 900 was longitudinal). This was achieved by unsealing the engine room box that had characterized the 99, where the engine was entombed in steel.

The structure of the car meant that a two-stage crumple zone was created – soft, less soft and then hard in terms of impact resistance versus energy absorption.

The 900 was extensively crash-tested. It was built to pass not just the head-on test, but also the offset or angled front-impact test. This was far harder to engineer for, and became law in Europe only in the 1990s, two decades after the 900 was built to pass it. According to Saab requirements, after a 30mph head-on or offset frontal impact, the doors must remain

Monte Carlo and the super-stylish Swede in five-door Turbo guise.

closed and in position – but easily opened with door handles and not special tools – and the windows must remain in their mountings. The 900 was one of the first cars to be built to pass the 30-degree offset crash test, and it did so with room to spare. In this respect, it was well ahead of subsequent legislation.

The engine mounts were also new. A prestressed rubber diaphragm mounted in a steel structure provided better NVH (noise, vibration, harshness) characteristics.

Rollover Protection and Pillars

Like the 99, the 900 had superb rollover protection. It also had foam blocks added to the doorbar-equipped doors. Extra floorpan cross-members – notably an underfascia cross beam – improved side-impact resistance.

The main structural problem with turning the 99 into the 900 lay with the windscreen pillars, or A posts. In the 99, they had formed the front of the cabin wall, stretching from the roof rail down to the sills and the rear of the front wheel arches. This unbroken support beam had been made of solid 2.5mm rolled steel and provided incredible rollover protection.

On the 900, Saab moved the footwells and wheel arches forward; there was no space for the windscreen pillars to run down to, as their previous tie on the back of the wheel arch had moved. Saab chopped the pillars off at scuttle height and welded them to the door uprights, where they met the inner wing rail and scuttle cross-member. A solid steel tie bar across the car, under the dashboard, was added. An impenetrable barrier had been forged once again. Special Z-shaped crush members were added to transfer forces down through the car's floorpan. As a result, the 900 was soft up front, to absorb impact, but harder towards the rear, to provide occupant survival space.

The front of the car's cage was built like a tank. As a result of an accident investigation, Saab also further reinforced the windscreen pillars with angled fillets in the mid-1980s, and beefed up the roof cross beams and cant rail.

Thicker steel was used for the sill box rails and the floor cross-members – enhancing intrusion resistance. The doors contained box-section anti-intrusion bars sited at the average height of car bumpers. Extra padding was put into the cabin and under-dashboard knee-roll impact padding catered for unbelted Americans.

Lights

For a short period, the new 900 came with 'day-running' lights, also used by Volvo. This safety device met Swedish legislation and in changing road conditions, with light turning to shade, it was easier to spot a car equipped with running lights than one without them. After several years, however, 'day-running' lights went out of favour and were dropped by both Volvo and Saab.

The 900's extensive range of safety features led to independent American accident investigation unit USHLDI naming the model 'safest mid-size car in the USA', from 1988–90.

STYLING CHANGES

Returning from a spell at Adam Opel AG in Germany, Bjorn Envall had taken over at Saab after the death of Sixten Sason, and had been responsible for the maturing of the 99 in the 1970s. The 900 was pure Envall – curved but not heavy-looking, classy but not weak-looking, it was a great mix of the Saab styling motifs that Sason and Envall had created over the years.

The early low, flat-front 900s represented a new beginning, but some versions still had old-fashioned chrome window trims and 'hub caps', and the early grilles were rather dated. Within just two years, Saab began to update the cars to a more modern style, and rationalized the model variants. They were soon dechromed across the range, being brought into line with the Turbo model.

Early cars also had the high-backed seats from the 99. Within eighteen months, Saab had redesigned the top of the front seats to incorporate a new headrest design. The interiors were finished in luxury-grade pleated velour.

Exterior

Body Shape

The 900 was launched as a five-door, with rear side 'opera' windows, and then a three-door version was added to the range. The four-door body and then the two-door body came along in the early and mid-1980s in a wide variety of specifications. In 1981, an elegant four-door saloon was offered, with a uniquely shaped rear windscreen that was typically Saab in so many ways. On the hatchback body, Envall used the design of the 99 Combi, complete with its airflow-tuned rear window that had been shaped to clean itself with air directed over it. A small lip spoiler also helped to keep the rear screen clean – a small but vital safety factor in bad conditions.

The 900's drag co-efficient was lower than that of the 99, helped by the extra length and boundary-layer airflow tuning.

Early three-door 900 Turbos came with 99 T 'Inca' wheels. This is a 1979 model.

99

The EMS badge lived on in the 900, complete with yet another set of alloy wheels.
This 1980 car had no spoilers.

1982: Four doors, steel wheel trims and a new look.

The car was also stable in crosswinds. The aerodynamic tuning included two aerodynamic vanes under the car on each side towards the rear axle. These caused airflow and pressure changes, which deliberately controlled and reduced turbulence both behind and under the car, and even tuned the drag envelope behind the car. The sunroof also had a small frontal lip, which was just enough to curve the localized boundary-layer airflow over the aperture without actually breaking the airflow. This reduced the drag and fuel economy penalty normally associated with an open roof or window.

The 900 also retained the 99's highly curved, low-drag, low-noise front windscreen. On the original model, the increased depth of the front screen enhanced the curve and, with its low front grille panel and blended-in lamps and bumpers, the 'flat-front' car had a 'swoopy' feel to it. By 1987, it had been shortened by nearly an inch at the front and given an attractive, slanted-back front grille and a lamp panel that was raked back 23 degrees, to improve airflow. On this 'slant-nose' 900, curved, one-piece bumper housings replaced the rather fussy side bumper to rubbing strip attachments.

The four-door 900 of 1981 was aimed at the more conservative or business buyer. Its rear end was totally new, and not derived from the 99, like the body shell of the three- and five-door 900s. It featured an elegant, swept boot line (and a large boot), and a

The quintessential 900 Turbo three-door.

Highlights of 900 Model History

1979
900 Chassis numbers: Swedish-9079100001-90791034858, 90792000001-90792004463;
Finnish-9079 6000001-90796004675
GL, GLS, EMS, GLE, Turbo trim levels
Three- and five-door
100bhp, 118bhp, 145bhp engines
GL cars – single–carburettor version with manual four-speed box
GLS – twin-carburettor, automatic option, injection engine
GLE – upgraded trim, manual or auto injection engine
EMS – sports trim, different wheel trims, injection engine
Turbo – manual only 145bhp (DIN)

1980
Redesigned seats with new adjustable headrest design
Larger tail lamps on hatchbacks, bootlid-mounted light clusters in board
Grilles rationalized

1981
Many technical spec revisions for 1981 model year cars in August 1980
Launch of booted four-door saloon and stretched Finlandia limousine
New front spoilers; revised side rear-view mirror design; wider side rubbing strips into bumper
links; four-spoke steering wheel; fifth speed to gearbox; H-series engine; revised idler shaft and
ancillaries; smaller turbo unit
900 S model in USA (EMS dropped in USA)
Four-door saloon as GL, GLE, Turbo
Saloon 75lb (33kg) lighter than hatch due to simpler rear-end construction

1982
200,000th 900 manufactured in June 1982, less than four years since launch
APC system launched in Sweden only
Central locking; wide-angle side rear-view mirror for driver; GLE trim designation dropped – GL;
asbestos-free brakes

1983
De luxe two-tone paint scheme on three-door Turbo models; leather trim; electric pack (popular in USA)
900i two-door model with 118bhp
Absestos-free brake specification; glass tint changed from green to bronze; new centre console
design; electric windows on some models; sunroof with electric pack/ leather trim option for first
time; accessory dials in console on EMS and Turbo models

1984
Electronic ignition (breakerless) across entire range
16-valve engine debuts on 900
GLi dropped; EMS deleted in some markets
Executive limousine (900 CD long-body four-door saloon) launched
New chrome grille; black rear valance; new three-spoke steering wheel design
European market (not UK) 'Aero' in Pearlescent Silver with Colorado Red leather interior

1985
900 Turbo 16S – first heavily revised 900
First body-addenda car with side/sill panels and under-bumper valances front and rear; engine

---

uprated to 175bhp (DIN); three-spoke wheels
European market (not UK), labelled 'Aero' (but not the slant-nosed 'Aero' sold in the UK in 1990)
USA, T16 tagged SPG (Special Performance Group)

1986
'Airflow' body kit introduced, and separate add-on larger rear spoiler, wheel-arch flares; replacement rear-wing cabin air extractor vane mouldings
900 Convertible model: first as Turbo, then as 900i

1987
Major styling surgery: 23-degree rake back to front end; new grille and headlamp styling with one-piece curved bumpers front and rear; overall length shortened by 2in (50mm); interior changes
'Airflow'-style body kit remoulded with integrated panels

1988
Two-door 900 T16 model launched, with new boot lip spoiler, three-spoke wheels, three-spoke steering wheel, body kit, and velour or leather trim; 175bhp
263 examples sold in UK before model dropped in 1990
Carlsson three-door 900 launched, with extra 10bhp

1990
900 SE models launched. Multi-spoked alloys, trim changes
Light-pressure 145bhp Turbo launched as 900 S

1991
True 'Aero' model launched, based on 175bhp full-boost T16 turbo. Badged as T16 'Aero'
Later low-pressure 'Aero', with revised lower panel cladding kit, and light-pressure turbo engine, was less powerful than T16 'Aero' (145bhp). This engine later fitted to 900 S model

1992
900i 'Aero', rare injected non-turbo model with 'Aero' body cladding/trim, listed by Saab UK

1993
31 March: final edition of Classic 900 in Turbo 'Ruby' guise. Air con, special seat trim, unique wheel finish, 185bhp as standard
End of 900 MkI production

highly unusual rear windscreen. The rear roof pillars, or C pillars, were totally redesigned, giving 30cm extra headroom. The side-panel air extractor vents of the 99 and 900 hatchbacks were moved up to the trailing edge of the C pillar.

Wheels and Tyres
The early three-door 900s in Turbo trim had 'Inca' wheels fitted, while turbine vane wheels were fitted to the five-door version. By 1982, a rationalization of wheel specification had taken place; the 'Inca' wheels were deleted and all Turbos came with the same wheels and tyres. By the mid-1980s, the 900 GLE had lost its brushed-steel wheel trims and taken to alloys. In the later years, 900s were offered with a series of attractive alloy wheels, from three-spoked, three-holed and turbine-style, to multi-spoked and dished 'US Turbo'-badged wheels with edge spokes. Rarest of all were the 'Super Inca' alloys, a stylistic derivative of the

The 1982 cars had wider rear lamps, with the extra units mounted in board on the tailgate. Note the 'APC System' and '5 Speed' badges.

original 'Inca' wheels on the 99 Turbo. The 'Super Incas' were three-spoked with ridged triangular sections.

In 1987, the newly launched 9000 range gave its attractive alloy wheels to the 900 Turbo range. The same car's seats also made it into the 900 range soon after.

Early 900 Turbos came with different tyre specifications – the five-door Turbos with the new Michelin TRX range on 180/65 rims, and the three-door Turbos with Pirelli P6 rubber on 195/60 rims.

Lamps and Mirrors

As with the 99, cars for the USA had to have different headlamps. US laws were satisfied by a smaller, square-sealed, beam-type unit mounted into the European-spec headlamp aperture. An extra lamp plate was added in board of the new square lamp lens – it worked but lacked the elegance of the original design.

Regular changes were made to the design of the 900's rear-view mirrors, mounted on the side doors. The first cars had small chrome mirrors mounted on stalks. The large 'elephant-ear' rear-view mirrors of 1983 were soon replaced, by 1985, by smaller, more aerodynamic, faired-in mirrors.

In the mid-1980s, extra rear lamps were added to the hatchback.

Paintwork and Body Kits
Dark or rich metallic paint on the Saab bodies really emphasized the strength of the sculptural statement of the 900. Some cars were produced in two-tone colour schemes, which seemed to lengthen the car even more. In 1983, a number of two-tone de luxe 900s were produced, with leather trim, US-style alloys, electric sunroof – and a price increase. They were rare cars and are still highly desirable.

In 1985, Saab's design centre worked to create a subtle body kit for the 900, which offered a concave curved lower sill, door/side panels with under-bumper valance and spoilers front and rear. This

---

Saab 900 Launch Prices

900 GL three-door £5,525
900 GLS three-door £5,775
900 GLS three-door auto £6,225
900 GLS five-door £5,995
900 GLS five-door auto £6,555
900 EMS (three-door only) £6,995
900 GLE (three-/five-door) £7,675
900 Turbo three-door £8,675
900 Turbo five-door £8,995

By 1990, the 900 range was priced from just under £15,000 to over £20,000.

---

created the 900 T16, which later became the definitive UK market 'Aero'. In 1989, Sweden's 'Aero' got a sports exhaust, a larger rear spoiler and revised air outlet covers. These features were offered in the UK as part of a styling kit range that started with the 'Airflow' body kit and 'Carlsson'-badged tweaks.

The basic 900 three-door flat-front car of 1985, with revised side rubbing strips and new wheel trims in brushed steel.

Workhorse Saab – the classic 900 five-door shape of 1985.

Interior

The 900's instruments and ancillary controls were found in a curved housing inspired by aircraft cockpit design. The dials were clear, the information was easy to assimilate, and rotary and push switches were sited in designated function zones. The radio was placed high so that the driver did not have to look away from the road for too long. A big impact-absorbing steering wheel and modular side-door trims added to the sense of Scandinavian style. A padded knee roll ran the width of the under-dashboard area, and the car also had heated orthopaedic seats and a pollen filter in the constantly driven cabin air system.

The early 900 Turbos had the large diagonal pleat/strip seat trim that had debuted on the 99 EMS. Within two years, in 1981, a new seat trim known as 'plush' had been introduced and the pleating strips were removed (although they continued to be hinted at in the stitching on top-of-the-range models). In 1985, a large box-pleated trim design was introduced across the range, which looked especially good in leather. The rear seat of the 900 saloon also featured advanced pocket-sprung construction – a first for Saab and, indeed, for any car.

Four- and five-door cars had 'add-on' door armrests, while two- and three-door cars had the armrests moulded into their one-piece door trims.

900 Development

900 GLE 1979
Engine:
Type:	four cylinders, 8 valves, Bosch fuel injection
Capacity:	1985cc
Max power:	118bhp/88Kw at 5,300rpm
Max speed:	106mph (170km/h)

Transmission:
Four-speed manual then optional five-speed box. Three-speed autobox option

Dimensions:
Original length with early extended bumpers 186.5in (4.8m)
Weight: 2,585lb (1,175kg)

900 Turbo 8-valve 1980
Engine:
Type:	four cylinders
Capacity:	1985cc
Max power:	145bhp/108Kw at 5,000rpm
Max speed:	120mph (195km/h)

Transmission:
Five-speed manual gearbox or three-speed auto

Dimensions:
Weight: 2,960lb (1,342kg)

900 Turbo 16S 1985
Engine:
Type:	Four cylinders, 16-valve head, two chain drive OHC, turbocharged (Garrett T3), water intercooler with additional cooling fan system
Capacity	1985cc
Max power	175bhp/130Kw at 5,000rpm
Max speed	135mph (212km/h)

Transmission:
Five-speed gearbox

Dimensions:
Weight with body kit: 2,965lb (1,346kg)
(900 T 'Ruby' of 1993 was lighter – no body kit)

On 900 light-pressure turbo LPT Model, reduced boost rating gave 145bhp DIN /107Kw; 16-valve gave over 10bhp more than corresponding injection engine

Throughout the life of the 900, seats, interior trims and centre consoles changed, but the dashboard design could not be bettered. Early cars had fake chrome trim strips around the instrument cluster and on the glovebox. The model trim designation, for example, 'GL', was painted in fake chrome style on the glovebox lid. All chrome-look trims were removed in 1986. Many cars had a cherrywood veneer dash kit fitted.

In 1981, a new four-spoke steering wheel was installed and a smart 1950s-style wood-rimmed steering wheel, with three aluminium spokes, was also a popular option.

ENGINEERING CHANGES

Throughout the 1980s, Saab improved the 900 with a series of engineering modifications. The developing character of the 900 was represented by a series of front grilles that were tried across the range (this feature was finally standardized in 1986). For the 1981 model year, a number of engineering changes were made to the entire 900 range. The revised H-series engine was reduced in weight by 26.5lb (12kg) with the removal of the idler shaft and drive gear. The turbo unit was also reduced in size and weight, being changed to a swing-type waste-gate function. The water pump was now driven by a belt and the oil pump and distributor were driven off the crankshaft. The fuel pump was pushrod-actuated. Non-turbo cars saw the compression ration rise from 9.2:1 to 9.5, offering better fuel consumption.

In 1981, a lower-priced 900 Turbo model was also available in Sweden. It was a three-door car that came without alloys and had standard specification tyres.

PRICES

At its launch, in 1979, the 900 was well priced, yet the prices of new cars rose significantly over the years, perhaps because the model remained in production for so long. By 1986, the 900 Turbo Convertible had hit the £20,000 mark in the UK.

Overseas Specification Differences

USA:
Max power:
Turbo 900
135bhp/100Kw at 5,000rpm (reduced bhp and torque output); 217Nm/22.1kgf/m at 3,000rpm; 0.5+-0.05 bar charge at 3,000rpm

91 octane lead-free fuel
Changes to firing point degree
Emission-control equipment including catalyst and Lambda system with EGR valve

Australia/Far East:
Max power:
non-Turbo 900
115bhp/85Kw at 5,500rpm; 167Nm/17.0kgf/m at 3,500rpm (reduced figures compared with European cars)

No engine oil cooler. No engine pre-heaters

By 1987, the four-door had gained the new slant nose, alloy wheels from the 9000 and the full Turbo trim kit. The rear windscreen was pure Saab in style.

900 Cabriolet of 1986; note the US-spec headlamp lenses.

The elegant Cabriolet with the roof up.

900 CABRIOLET OR CONVERTIBLE

The idea of a soft-top or convertible 900 had been circling round the Saab design centre for some time, but it required financial resources. Could a five-year-old car possible be facelifted profitably into a convertible? Most marketing men and motor industry accountants would have said 'No'.

The car was initially labelled '900 Cabriolet' and launched as a concept car based on the newer two-door 900 body shell. The American Sunroof Company (ASC), with years of experience of creating and converting other manufacturers' bodies to roofless designs, wanted to test the market for such a car. Envall drew an idea, keeping the rising body line, but creating a neat stowage system and shroud for the soft top, which would fold down into its boot storage area. The windscreen pillars were re-angled to 45 degrees and the A pillars and windscreen frame were thickened and tied down to reinforced sills and side-members. This structure restored some of the torsional rigidity that would be lost in taking the 900's roof off. Safety was not compromised and the car satisfied Saab's extensive tests.

The car weighed in at just under 3,000lb (1,365kg) because of the heavy reinforcements and electric roof gear. Performance was affected, so Envall came up with an interesting aerodynamic 'lip' that ran around the rear of the cabin and acted as a spoiler and airflow tuner when the hood was folded, and when it was up. This feature was totally unique in the history of convertible design. On later models it was extended around the whole of the convertible's cabin aperture.

The folding roof came with a real glass rear windscreen – a first on any convertible car. This windscreen, along with the roof, was electrically managed and slid down into its own protective storage area behind the rear cabin scuttle. Furthermore, it was fully retractable with the roof up.

The first soft-top 900 was finished in white and exhibited at US and European motor shows in 1983. The first cars became available in 1985. The Saab/ASC convertible was a 'flat-front' 900 with the full 175bhp turbo engine with intercooler. The interior was leather-lined and the roof doubly insulated. The car immediately injected extra life into the range. (Little did Saab's managers know that a privately built one-off soft-top 900 already existed in Sweden, put together by a Saab fan in 1983!)

Following the initial reaction, Saab decided to proceed with production and the car was a hit world wide. Later, the car was restyled with the 'slant nose' that had been applied to all 900s. In 1990, a cheaper, non-turbo injected version was also made available. 'Aero'-style body panels were also applied to some models of the convertible to create a convertible 16S model.

At a UK price of £25,000 and as a $50,000 dollar car in the USA, the top-of-the-range convertibles became the flagship cars for Saab. In all, over 10,000 soft-top 900s were made and sold worldwide.

Lynx Engineering

Lynx Engineering, an established British firm with a history of creating convertible versions of fine cars, put together a rare short-run conversion of the two-door 900 shell. Choosing the 900 because of its high torsional stiffness, they created a removable targa roof, leaving side braces and B posts in place for rollover protection. A folding hood was constructed for the rear roof section and new laminated and removable side windows were made. Lynx charged £4,000 to carry out the conversion on a 900.

MODEL VARIANTS AND SPECIAL EDITIONS

The early range included GL, GLS, GLE and Turbo models, identified by differences in chrome trims, wheel hubcap designs and grilles.

During its life, the 900 was used as a basis for several special editions. Some of the 900 model names varied. For example, there are two distinct 'Aero' types, with the T16S as forerunner in the UK, and in Italy, APC cars were badged 'EP'. The 'Airflow' models later shared their body kits with the 'Carlsson', while the final, full-bore 'Ruby' model came with no body additions at all.

1988 two-door 900 T16S; 1990 three-door full-bore 'Aero' T16S; 1991 'Aero S' LPT

The two-door 900 body shell was fitted with the 16-valve turbo engine, and came with boot spoiler, lower panels and three-spoke alloys. Only 263 cars were sold in the UK from its launch in 1988 to its demise in 1990.

A car of the same spec, but with three-door shell and the later UK market 'Aero' body cladding, was sold in Europe as an 'Aero'. T16s became full-bore Aero T16s in 1990. A light-pressure 'Aero S' was also available.

Early flat-front 'Aero' cars were sold only in mainland Europe as 'Aero' in 1986.

900 'Carlsson'

This UK market special was named after rally legend Eric Carlsson. Based on the three-door shell and launched in 1990, it had an uprated 1985cc turbocharged engine with APC, and 1985bhp pumping out through twin chrome exhausts. A special body kit consisting of front and rear under-bumper aprons, and side skirts based on the 'Airflow' body kit, distinguished it from the T16 or 'Aero' body kit. Available in black, white or red, the first batch had enlarged rear spoilers, rear infill lamp panels, 'Carlsson' stickers, and red side stripes. The car also had lower suspension.

In its second year, the 'Carlsson' gained suede- and leather-trimmed seats and, in 1992, a changed wheel specification. Many came with a three-spoke, wood-rimmed, Nardi-style steering wheel.

900 CD (Long Body)

Launched in 1983, to take advantage of the so-called 'executive' car market, the 900 CD was available only in the new four-door booted body shell. It had longer rear side doors and Saab had also changed the tooling of the front doors, at some expense. The front and rear side doors each had a 100mm extension, with the full 200mm extension being incorporated at the B post. Despite the additions, it was only 45lb (20kg) heavier than the original.

With its increased rear legroom, the 900 CD was ideal as a company limousine or upmarket chauffeur-driven car. The 900 CD had no cramped occasional-use foldaway seats and looked nothing like a hearse. According to Saab, it offered 'a new type of limousine in which the yardstick of elegance is no longer the folding extra seats or space for eight people. It is distinguished in a different, more modern, more efficient way.' In other words, it was a proper limousine, rather like the Citroen CX Prestige.

The 900 was provided with luxury trim and lavishly equipped with every option available. Its turbo engine (with APC) was

A range of VIP limousines from Saab Valmet used the extended body of the 900 CD, note the longer front and rear doors.

ABOVE: *T16 S cars were badged 'Aero' in Scandinavia and Germany in 1986, with a body kit in black or paint colour. The three-spoke alloys were new for the model. British 'Aero' cars were first sold as T16 S and then as 'Aero'. A later 'Aero 16S' and a light-pressure turbo model 'Aero' were also sold.*

LEFT: *900 interior view.*

BELOW: *The facelifted five-door 900 LPT Turbo of 1990, minus alloys.*

The four-door saloon in 1983 featured Turbo trim, spoilers and 'turbine'-style wheels.

The 1986 three-door 900i came without a rear spoiler. This model sported the Saab-Scania roundel badge on its rump.

mated to a three-speed autobox.

An early version for the Swedish market had the attractive jet engine-styled 'turbine blade' wheels from the original 900 Turbo range, but the British versions of 1984 came with a different alloy wheel design.

The 900 Valmet Limousine was an even longer-bodied official-function stretched VIP limo, based on the 900 CD and built in Finland by Valmet.

Anniversary Editions

The 'Tjugofem', a special edition of 300 cars based on the 1985 900i, marked Saab's twenty-fifth anniversary in Britain. The Saab GB special came with silver paint, side stripes, colour-keyed grille, lower front spoiler and Turbo-style alloys. Interior upgrades included rear head restraints, electric windows, electric mirrors, tinted glass, centre console and a numbered gear knob. The car also had a rear infill panel between the lights, and a rear boot spoiler.

Although labelled as a 'Jubilee' car, the 'Tjugofem' should not be confused with the later 900 'Jubilee' models that marked Saab's fiftieth anniversary in 1988. These were mainly three-door shells in Odorado Grey with special wheel trims, leather seats and Saab house-colour side stripes.

In 1989, Saab launched the 900 Turbo 'Anniversary', based on the three-door 900 Turbo and designed to celebrate the tenth year of Turbo production. The car came with black paint, striping, a whale-tail spoiler and 'minilite'-style wheels under wheel-arch flares. The interior featured electric mirrors, sunroof and a four-spoke steering wheel.

Other Specials

One of the earliest special editions of the 900 was the 900 'GOLD'. Launched in 1981, the car featured a Turbo model interior and special Turbo-type suspension settings. Its graphics package

The 1987 facelift cleaned up the car's lines and integrated the bumper units into the overall styling.

The definitive 900 T.

1992 'Aero', with the attractive three-hole alloys that it shared with the revised 9000 range.

ABOVE: Non-'Aero' Turbo at the end of 900 production – the alloy wheels are different again!

LEFT: The 900 was best known for its narrow-windscreen 'turret'-styled look.

BELOW: The classic profile of the 900 three-door, arguably the purest-looking of the 900 body styles.

ABOVE: *A quintessential Saab 900 two-door of the late 1980s.*

RIGHT: *Saab's own multi-spoked alloy wheel, as found on the 900 Turbo and SE models in 1990.*

BELOW: *The new 900 two-door shell of 1985 with S-pack trim kit, including minilite-style alloy wheels. The 900 had over twelve wheel designs and trims in its lifetime.*

featured gold coachlines and gold-coloured 'minilite'-type spoked wheels.

The limited edition 900 GLE of September 1981 was less well known. The cars were mostly four-door saloons, finished in metallic blue, pine green or black, highlighted with gold side stripes and 'minilite' alloy wheels. They cost £9,165 in the UK, or £270 more than the standard model.

The 900 XS was a little-publicized Saab special edition based on the 900i. It came with special multi-spoked alloys, a rear-lamp decor panel and leather trim. Most were finished in dark metallic green or blue and came with five doors. Only 200 or so were sold in 1991–92.

Launched in May 1990, the 900 SE was based on the 900i, but was kitted out as a luxurious top-of-the-range model. It had the rare 900 walnut veneer fascia inlay, leather trim, rear wash/wipe and cross-spoked alloys. It was available only in metallic Iridium Blue, with a fine gold coachline down each side. The 900 SE came with ABS and an engine that gave 133bhp. The British market received 300 such SE models.

The Saab 900 'Airflow' was created in 1987 using the special body kit from Saab UK mounted on the three-door Turbo shell. The kit was later used on the 'Carlsson' model (see page 112).

The 900 'Silver Arrow' was a special edition for the Dutch market, based on the two-door 900i body shell, but with Turbo-style alloys, special logos and stripes, chrome grille and a rear lip spoiler.

The Cabrio in Monte Carlo with the roof neatly stowed in its clever housing behind the rear seats.

By 1988, the facelifted 900 with slant nose had made the 'Aero' even smarter.

The 900 'Ruby' was the ultimate Classic 900. Offered in mica metallic Ruby Red, it used the 185bhp turbo engine, but kept the pure lines of the 900, with no body kit. Features included air conditioning, Zegna wool seat trim inserts, lowered suspension, three-hole alloys with unique graphite finish and the car was fully loaded with electrically powered options. The list price of £19,995 made it the most expensive 900 ever and the model is now highly prized.

The Saab 900 Friction Tester was a special edition of the three-door body shell, fitted with a tester for airport runways. Data-processing equipment allowed analysis of the runway surface in terms of skid, water-planing and braking conditions. Painted in high-visibility colours, several hundred of the cars were sold worldwide to airport authorities.

As with the 99, Saab created a van version of the 900 by fitting steel window blanks into the side of three-door models,

and a floor and bulkhead in place of rear seats. They were sold in Denmark, and a few were copied and built in the UK by Saab dealerships. One-off 900 pick-ups have also been built by individuals.

Conversions and Upgrades

A number of companies, notably in Britain and Sweden, carried out modifications to the 99 and the 900. British company Abbott Racing of Essex was known for its handling, suspension and engine upgrades to the Classic 900. The most significant changes were made to the steering and suspension settings.

Sports exhausts and re-trimming also identified the 'Specials' from Trent Saab. This British company is best known for its engine upgrade packages on the Classic 900. Their T-power turbo conversion yielded 220bhp for the 900 T16. The kit included a remapped APC 'brain' 0.5 bar wastegate with a recirculating turbo dump

---

Saab in America

The aviation heritage of Saab is once again dominant in its overseas history. In Great Britain, Saab as an importer of Swedish cars was set up as a company by an ex-Royal Air Force officer. In America, another aviation fanatic, Ralph Millet, himself a pilot who owned an aeronautical company, first became associated with Saab as early as 1951 when he investigated importing the 92 to the country. At this time, the VW Beetle and small European cars were becoming very popular, and only the Saab's two-stroke engine handicapped it.

By 1956, Trggve Holm had met with Millet and legend has it that Holm sent a handful of 93s over to America without much hope from Millet of making any impact. Yet with a stand at the 1956 New York auto show – including a display of a cut-away, sectioned 93 and one of the rare, Sonnet 1 two-seat roadsters – the Saab name and the Saab look made a mark. 250 cars were soon shipped across the Atlantic. An incredible class win in a major American rally – the Great American Mountain Rally of 1956, through the snow clad eastern states – launched the Saab name in America; later on, Saab also triumphed in the hot and high Baja 1000 rally in New Mexico.

As early as 1958, the man who was to become the doyen of Saab's American operation, Robert Sinclair, joined the company. Years later, after career moves within the motor industry, Sinclair, a true 'petrol head', would return to oversee Saab America, and the Saab 900 convertible, via the American Sunroof Company, was his pet project. Back in the 1960s, Saab Motors which was not then incorporated in America, became Saab of America. By the 1968 model year, the V4-engined cars gave Saab a new lease of life in the American market and paved the way for the 99, which itself laid solid foundations for the 900 when it in turn appeared in 1979.

The 99 three-door Combi became the Wagonback in the United States, with special trim, badges and wheel trims; Saab sold over 20,000 cars a year in America during this period. Sales fell in the late 1970s, but picked up again with the advent of the 99 Turbo and the 900 range. By 1986, Saab sold nearly 50,000 cars a year in the USA – no mean achievement. Each month saw a rise in the sales figures: these were heady days for Saab in the USA and it was the 900 that made them possible.

With Robert Sinclair's interest in motor sport, Saab of America became involved in various promotional events for the 900, this reaching from the age of the 99 Turbo, through the NASCAR production stock racing series, and on to the new 900 with the Talledaga record-breaking endurance and speed runs. This was all good marketing material for Saab and Sinclair, who worked closely with Sten Helling of Saab America and Sten Wennlo in Sweden to expand the Saab brand in America.

Post-General Motors, Saab has re-emerged as a quality brand and a premier badge in America, but few will forget the days of the US-spec 900 Turbos of the mid-1980s. Some, trimmed in two-tone paint with Scottish Bridge of Weir leather seats, were the ultimate 900s; for many, the three-door cars in black or a four-door saloon in metallic crimson, green or silver blue, trimmed in plush pleated velour or pamir leather, with alloy wheels and sunroofs, were the strongest statement of Saabs, an alternative to BMW and Mercedes. The American motoring press loved these cars and took them to their hearts as sporting performance saloons par excellence. To this day, despite the new GM lineage, Saabs remain what they always were to the Americans: something different, something Saab.

---

valve, rising rate fuel pressure regulator and a steel air-extractor exhaust modification. The kit gave a huge increase in mid-range torque and knocked 2 seconds off the 0–60mph figure. The turbo lag was also reduced. Crucially, the all-important 50–70mph 'overtaking' segment time was cut to just 4.1 seconds.

At Solstad's Bil, based in Roke, Sweden, Robert Solstad started creating ultra-long wheelbase conversions on Saab chassis back in 1982. The firm produced pick-ups, transporters and funeral cars, particularly a 99 flatbed pick-up and the attractively styled 900 Turbo transporter, with its six wheels and swept cab styling.

The EV-1, Bjorn Envall's vision of the future.

EV1 – SHOW CAR SPECIAL

In 1985, Bjorn Envall designed a vision of the future of which his old boss Sixten Sason would have been proud. The swoopy, glass-topped experimental car was based on the underpinnings of the 900 Turbo of that model year. Built in less than six months in steel, it had a curved windscreen and upswept tail; it was pure Saab. Underneath the bonnet lurked a 285bhp development of the Saab engine. The impact-absorbing front and rear sections of the car were built of aerospace-grade aramid fibre. Side-impact protection was enhanced with composite carbon-fibre reinforced doors. The solar-powered ventilation and dehumidifying system was particularly interesting – solar cells were mounted in the roof glass.

The EV1 was a big star on the international concept-car scene and an excellent advertisement for Saab and its design centre.

The longevity of the Saab 900 was quite simply extraordinary; as a model, it was outlived only by those two exemplars of motoring history, the Mini and the 2CV. The 99 had run from 1968 to 1984, then its successor lasted from 1979 to 1993, when production of the Classic Saab 900 – the last real Saab, according to some – ended. Despite being based on a car designed in 1977, which had its roots in 1961, the boat-shaped 900 with its aircraft-style windscreen was, and is, an icon of individualistic style.

8   Competition Cars

RALLYING THE 92-96

Despite a lack of power, the Saab 92-96s were the perfect rally cars. They were nimble, small and incredibly strong, and the rally driver could turn them over again and again without any problems. Indeed, Eric Carlsson soon acquired the Swedish nickname 'Carlsson – *pa tacket*', or 'on the roof'. The two-stroke 92-96 took on the big Healeys of the day, with just over 800cc against 3 litres, and the addition of the V4 engine made the Saab even more competi-

tive. The fact that the little Saab had drum brakes and limited stopping power only added to its 'press-on' nature.

The first Saab rally success occurred just a few months into the life of the 92, in 1949, when an early model was driven to first place in the Circuit of Ostergotland Endurance Rally by K.V. Svedburg. In early 1950, Rolf Mellde and Svedburg, and women drivers Greta Molander and Margareta von Essen, entered the Monte Carlo Rally, and both cars finished the event.

The 96 rally car in its element.

In the early 1950s, the Saab engine test department took over the preparation and specification of rally cars. Although special engines were built for the rally cars, the standard Saab body shell was so strong that few modifications were needed to the rest of the car.

For more than a decade, the two-stroke Saabs stormed the world rally scene, and established a legendary reputation at club level. The first Great American Mountain Rally of 1956 was won by a Saab, driven by Bob Wheman and Louis Braun; Rolf Mellde came sixth. Carlsson stormed the Baja 1000 in California and, on two occasions, came second in the East African Safari rally.

Carlsson and his regular co-drivers and navigators, Gunnar Palm, Torsten Aman and Walter Karlsson, simply swept the board in European rallying. Carlsson won the Monte Carlo Rally three times, from 1961 to 1963 (co-driven by Gunnar Haggbom and then Gunnar Palm) and triumphed in the RAC rallies of 1960–63 (co-driven by Stuart Truner, John Brown, and David Stone). In total, Carlsson took the rally Saabs to ten European Championship rally wins from 1959 to 1967. In 1959, two Saab 93Bs were even entered into the Le Mans 24-hour race. The car driven by Sture Nottrop and Gunnar Bengstsson came twelfth overall and second in class, one of only thirteen finishers of the race.

RALLYING THE 99

Saab's Rally Department

Saab's impressive rallying reputation, won with the 92-96 series cars, meant that the 99 had a lot to live up to. Many wondered whether anything could match the earlier models. How could the 99, which was so much bigger, win rallies? And it was not only bigger. It was also heavier, harder to steer, and certainly not as nimble. Changing direction, and throttle- or brake-steering were much more difficult.

The 99 may have looked unpromising as a rally car, yet it worked. There were early problems – notably with driveshafts and gearboxes – but the 99, first in EMS and then in Turbo guise, eventually cracked the rally act and even became world champion. And if all that were not enough, Saab's reputation lived on in the rally and saloon car racing of the even larger 900.

The foundations of the 99's rallying success were laid in the 1960s in Saab's rally department at Trollhättan, led by Bosse 'Bo' Hellborg. The transition was not easy and many hard lessons were learned, but Saab was persistent. The company's rally department evolved during the heyday of the 96 and 99 until it had acquired a ten-car preparation bay, a team of twenty mechanics and a competition budget. Under long-established manager Bo Hellborg was 'Baby Bo' Swaner, who went on to head the Saab 99 Turbo rally team.

Having made the decision to rally the 99, Saab entered the car into various rallies in stock form, with minor upgrades. A few privateers made headway, but real progress was made only when Saab rebuilt the standard 2-litre 99 EMS engine. A revised cylinder head, forged and specially machined parts, higher compression ratio and 16 valves were all incorporated into the engine, which was reputed to reach 200bhp, and fitted into a two-door EMS shell in late 1975. The car's first competition outing was the Boucles de Spa rally in Belgium in February 1976, when it was driven by Stig Blomqvist.

Champion rally driver Stig Blomqvist and the 1979 two-door 99 Turbo rally car.

A series of problems followed, but Saab fought back and went on to win the Swedish winter rally of April 1977.

Rallying the New Turbo

Saab announced a rally programme for its new Turbo at the 1978 Swedish motor show. Initially based on a three-door body shell, the car had a reputed 240bhp turbocharged engine. Uprating a competition engine to this degree was rare and risky. Reliability would obviously be a problem, particularly in hotter countries.

Boosted from 145bhp to 240bhp at a low 5,700rpm peak, the turbo offered faster stage times, but was more limited on slow

stages. Rally cars need low-rev torque in muddy and slippery conditions, rather than a high-revving super boost that works like an on/off switch. The 99 Turbo rally car had to be tuned to be tractable. The main weakness of the 16-valve EMS engine installation was that it needed to be spinning at 4,000rpm to be effective, whereas the new turbo unit came on song at 2,500rpm, which was excellent on slippery and hilly rally stages. Fewer gear changes were a side benefit of this engine's capabilities. The turbo was boosted to 1.6 bar instead of 0.8 bar in the production car. Gear ratios were changed to rally special stage choices. A modified waste-gate and special cooling fan for the turbo unit helped keep things in check.

Painted in jet black with zig-zagged side stripes in the Swedish national colours of blue and yellow, the car came with full roll cage, fire equipment, extra lamps, 'minilite'-type wheels, and navigator's storage space and instruments mounted on the front glove-box. The team of drivers for the two-car team were Stig Blomqvist with co-drive Bjorn Cederberg, and Per Eklund with co-driver Hans-Eric Sylvan. The Saab rally team also operated cars tuned to other championship groupings in Sweden and Europe and rotated its drivers among its cars. Simo Lampinen and Tapio Raino were other notable names among the Saab works rally team drivers. Mike Bennion and Will Townsend, mechanics from Saab GB, joined the service crew for the international series events.

From early 1977, the Saab EMS team had linked up with Swedish caravan maker Polar to create 'Team Polar', which competed under Polar sponsorship in the international rally competition with the 16-valve 99 EMS.

By 1978, the 99 Turbo was out on its own, with the two-door 99 rally car that was to lead to Blomqvist's world championship success. The two-door 99 was stiffer than the three-door body and lighter by 90lb (40kg). The engine was boosted to 240bhp and then up to 285bhp for 1979. Per Eklund had left Saab to drive the Triumph TR7 V8, so it was Stig Blomqvist who drove the Saab dealer team's three-door 99 Turbo in the 1979 Mintex rally – and won.

Blomqvist and Cederberg winning the 1979 Swedish rally on special wheels for icy conditions.

Blomqvist and Cederberg speeding through the snow in the 99 Turbo.

Blomqvist had previously won the Swedish rally in 1979, competing against major factory teams and scoring the first win on the international rally scene for a turbocharged car. For 1980, Saab and Blomqvist tackled over forty rallies in the Group 2 class in Sweden, Germany and Britain. Ola Stromberg and

Blomqvist used Group 2 cars in various races, while Stromberg also competed in Group 1 races with the 99 EMS.

Clarion car audio sponsored the team for 1981, but in 1982 Saab pulled out of rallying, following a series of failures with the cars. Rallies in hot climates had revealed the heat-soak and cooling problems that led to the intercooler and water-injection devices later seen on production turbos. Power steering also found its way under the already crowded bonnets of the rally cars.

Saab had created the 16-valve EMS around the 'homologation' rules, under which 100 examples of a production-based, but specially modified model had to be made. In this way, rally cars, although 'tweaked', remained quite closely related to the factory versions. After the advent of the 99 Turbo, the body overseeing international rallying decided to make some changes. Factories were allowed to build a series of special, one-off rally cars, which bore little resemblance to the road-going versions of the same brand name. Rally cars turned into prototype specials with huge non-standard powerplants and every

modification possible. The costs were huge and only those car makers prepared to invest millions in rallying would survive. The new rules also specified that 400 such cars would need to be made for homologation. It was the death knell for the Saab works rally team.

Privateers

Privateers continued to make a success of rallying the 99 in EMS and Turbo guises. In Britain, John Harrison drove his 99 EMS to fame with navigator Richard Burdon in many British club events (and continues to do so). His 99 benefited from a competition gearbox and limited slip differential, all developed outside Saab and long after the works team shut up shop.

Saab 99 Turbo Rally Car

Engine:

Type:	four cylinders
Capacity:	1985cc
Compression ratio:	6:5:1
Output:	246bhp at 6,000rpm
Max revs:	7,000rpm
Max torque:	236lb/ft
Turbocharger:	Garret AiResearch T3 at max boost of 1:6 bar
Performance:	0–60mph 7.0 secs; 0–100mph 14.58 secs
Top speed:	115mph (184km/h)

Transmission: strengthened four-speed box with limited slip differential

Wheels:	'minilite'-type alloy
Tyres:	Dunlop
Shock absorbers:	Bilstein gas dampers
Electrics.	Bosch
Oil:	Castrol

Weight 2,425lb (1,102kg) (two-door shell approx 40lb/18kg lighter)

Body: three-door hatchback. Full roll cage and brace bars, suspension mounting reinforcements. Fuel tank of 16.94 gallons in luggage compartment with safety shield. (Later moved to boot in two-door rally-car shell.)

Spec changes to brakes, exhaust, suspension, electrics, gearbox.

In 1979, Dave and Joan Martin privately rallied their 99 with sponsorship help from Saab dealer Alexanders, ICI, Duckhams, Pirelli and Ferodo. The car featured uprated brakes and suspension, changes to the driveshafts, strengthening to the front crossmember, seam welding to parts of the shell, a lighter fibreglass bonnet, stronger final drive and a revised exhaust. Theirs was the only 99 on the rally circuit outside the works team at the time.

In the same year, Phil Davies of Bolton Saab entered the Welsh Rally, while the Saab Owners Club followed the race in its Saab GB-supplied 99 Combi.

In 1985, Dave Broadbent and Barry Rowson entered a 99 in a series of British club races.

In Scandinavia, the less powerful 8-valve 99 EMS provided many Swedes with privateer entry into Swedish club-level rallying, and the Finns created their own 99 rally club team. In 1978, the 99 won all three classes of the Swedish national rally championships. In 1978, Stig Blomqvist took a standard 99 EMS to rally in Canada and won, beating many more powerful cars.

Saab employee Mike Bennion entered a 175bhp 99 Turbo in the 182/3 Monroe Production Saloon Car championship.

From the beginning, Saabs were popular in Australia and there are still a number of companies specializing in the brand, such as Saab Automotive in Brisbane, run by John Rues. Ian Ferguson entered his Classic 99 EMS, prepared by Saab Automotive, in a series of historic races based on Australia's pre-1975 classic racing series. Dave Elund of Saab Automotive built a circuit racer from a carbon-fibre 900 replica body shell with widened wings, with a 350 cubic inch Chevy engine installed. Former Formula One ace Alan Jones also had a Saab 900 Turbo for his own private use.

RALLYCROSS AND AUTOCROSS

At the same time as Saab was achieving international rally success, the British went rallycross mad with the 99, which became a real favourite on the UK rallycross scene. A Saab-sponsored rallycross 99, with 'Saab Finance' stickers, was driven by Will Gollop (and fettled by Tim Skinner) in the 1982 British rallycross championship. From 1977, Gollop had entered a 16-valve EMS but he soon took the Turbo to the mud. He had many rallycross wins at national level, notably Group A wins at Lydden Hill and Snetterton, and the overall championship.

With Saab sponsorship, in 1982, the team had wider resources via the Saab Finance rallycross team. Lyndon Fraser, the team's co-campaigner, prepared the 99's bodywork and suspension. Several of the car's panels were made in fibreglass to reduce weight, and the car was 616lb (280kg) lighter than a road-going 99 T. The Garret turbocharger was changed to a Schwitzer turbo and the car was able to reach 265bhp.

Over a decade later, the 99 was still being campaigned on the grass tracks of the British autocross world. Saab Owners Club members Ian Scott and Ken Bell took over Malcolm Dickinson's two-door 99 autocross car and added a water-injected 900 turbo engine, a quicker steering rack and revised suspension. With 201bhp and mud to drive on, the grass-driven 99 was 'interesting' to drive by all accounts.

RACING IN THE 900

With the demise of the production 99 and the arrival of the new 900 in 1979, Saab had to review its approach to rallying. The 900

The quintessential 99 rally car.

The 99 Turbo rally car in its element. Note the special snow wheels and tyres.

was hardly suitable for rallying, being even bigger and heavier than the 99. Yet, it has had a rally career at the hands of club members, and also entered saloon car racing in a sponsored series and achieved success.

In the UK, Saab dealer Beechdale formed the Beechdale Rally Team following success in the Turbo Challenge series. With a three-door and a two-door 900, the Beechdale team was a highly credible, sponsored professional outfit, with a full mobile service team. The team achieved many excellent class placings, notably in the RAC rally between 1989 and 1994. Drivers included Ola Stromberg, Will Gollup, John Wheatley, and Dave and Ian Wood.

Saab UK supported the saloon car series, notably through the Saab Turbo Mobil Challenge of 1988, and a series of national 900 races contested by individual dealer- and team-supported cars. The two-door race-prepared car of Saab dealer Haymill, driven by Charles Tippet, made many headlines, as did the cars driven by Tony Dron, James Latham, Lionel Abbott, Gerry Marshall, Andy Dawson and John Lewellyn.

In Sweden, the 900 made good progress at club level and was a keen high-speed 'ice' machine in the hands of driver Ola Stromberg and Tina Thorner.

In the USA, a series of challenges took place under the 'Team Saab' umbrella, with 900 Turbos competing in track endurance races. The 900 Turbo of Complete Saab of Woodstock, Georgia, achieved headlines for Saab on a number of occasions. In 1980, the car won an endurance race for stock-specification saloon cars, covering 1,850 miles (2,970km) in 24 hours, with only tyres and brakes needing to be changed. The team of drivers was made up of Bill Fishburne, Don Knowles, and John Dinkel and Joe Risz of *Road and Track* magazine.

Success in the series gave the 900 range and the Saab brand valuable publicity in the USA, at a time when Saab could no longer trumpet the rallying wins that had helped to create its name.

9 Buying a Classic Saab

This is not a definitive buyer's guide, but brings together personal experience and knowledge from the Saab Owners Club of Great Britain, with special thanks to Richard Elliot, technical advisor to the Saab Owners Club UK.

Saabs are known for their longevity and it is not rare to find 99s and 900s that have done well over a quarter of a million miles. Many reach 175,000 miles on their original engine and gearbox, and 300,000 miles on the 2-litre engine is a real possibility. On 7 February 2001, *Autocar* magazine featured two second-hand Saabs with mileages of 197,000 and 200,000 miles. The first, a 14-year-old 900 Turbo, was still on its original engine and gearbox, and, notably, still had its original turbo! The Saab Owners Club in the UK has over twenty 900s on its books, with mileages of between 200,000 and 295,000; many are still on their original engines and gearboxes. One example has so far covered 395,000 miles without major rebuild.

It was notable, too, that both *Autocar* examples had full service histories. Saabs do need regular servicing, but the cars have never suffered significantly from factory production-related defects. In the mid-1970s, clutch installations gave problems on 99s and the early cylinder-head design is a known problem area. Similarly, rot behind the rear seats and moisture in the headlamps is a recognized design-related failing. Yet, in comparison with the average car, Saabs are relatively problem-free.

Unlike some front-driven cars, Saabs do not quickly wear out their driveshafts. However, depending on the model and brand choice, it can be quite expensive to keep the Turbos supplied with grippy but soft front tyres.

Saabs do not look like any other car, and they do not rust like any other car... but they do rust, although at a rate that is different from the average tin-box car.

Buying a used Saab is a fairly safe proposition, but it requires careful thought. Look for as much Saab service history as possible, or a known non-franchised Saab specialist record. Certain features on the Saab 99 and 900 (see below) need to be have been ticked off, too. Imports are identified by badging and trim specification. This may be significant – for example, the batteries on many 900s sold in hot regions such as the Middle East and Far East had to be moved to the boot, because heat soak from the turbo boiled the battery acid.

ENGINE

Although Saab made many changes to the Triumph design of head-to-block joining, early 1709cc and 1854cc engines were prone to warped heads, often due to early cooling problems. Gaskets on early cars can therefore be difficult to change, a problem addressed by Saab's 2-litre engine revamp. Water pumps also need to be watched on earlier and later engines; tricky water pump replacement can be made easier with a special tool. Check the radiator carefully;

they had to work hard and can easily cause problems (the cars with the extra 'nostril'-style under-grille vents were better in this respect).

Camshaft wear is rare, since all the toolings were heavy-duty spec.

Timing chains are noisy but should not rattle excessively.

Exhaust manifold problems were known and modifications were made. Be wary of fitting cheap second-rate exhausts to a 99 or 900. Single-piece exhaust manifolds are prone to cracking; the later two-stage design is much easier to source and fit to earlier cars than an original.

Sticking valves and noisy camshafts also occurred, but after so many years, most 99 engines should have been attended too. The thing to look for is a record of regular, 6,000-mile services – regular oil changes are the key to long engine life.

Many modifications were made between engine types on the later 900 (which had a 10,000-mile service interval), but the head-gasket problems remained. On later cars with APC and intercoolers, look out for signalling failures and electronic interference. If the engine has 16 valves that means there is more to monitor in the alloy head too.

TURBO ENGINE

The Saab turbo engine underwent changes to the valves, pistons and crank, and, of course, it had a turbo unit bolted on. The turbo unit usually lasted for 50,000 to 75,000 miles, depending on its treatment. Some 99s and many 900s reached over 150,000 miles on their original turbos and engine heads. Look for bills and receipts for replacements.

The biggest bug-bear of the turbo unit was turbo-bearing failure or seal failure, signalled by smoke spurting out of the back of the car under load. Take a good look at the waste-gate function; sticking ones are difficult to fix and can overboost the head. The turbo units on oil-cooler cars tended to last longer and some owners tried to fit larger versions under the bonnet of their 99.

The sodium-treated valves can fail and are expensive to replace. As with the normally aspirated cars, the timing gear will rattle. If the rattle becomes really loud, the engine will have to come out.

Water-injection cars are rarer. The unit, and notably its hoses, needs to be checked carefully.

Many 900 Turbos have been modified to over 200bhp. This puts extra strain on the engine and gearbox and notably on the driveshafts and steering. Such cars must be checked out for any problems.

99 Turbos also went through a period where they went off-tune before their next scheduled service (again, although the turbo was good, the car needed regular servicing). 900 turbos units, particularly the later ones, were better and more durable, especially in low-boost variant. By this time, the 16-valve head was in use and many other technical changes had been undertaken.

Some enthusiast owners change their car's oil every 3,000–5,000 miles and monitor the gearbox oil weekly. (Note: the operating temperatures of the turbo mean that oil blackens quickly.)

GEARBOX

The main focus with the 99 and 900 has to be the gearbox. Many 99s and 900s, perfectly sound in other departments, have met an early end due to the prohibitive cost of repairing this item. It is an essential area of concern. Some gearboxes are trouble-free for over 150,000 miles, while others become truculent long before that mileage.

Saab 99 Paint Shades

Originals and additions by model year.

1969:	Toreador Red, Brown Beige, Sea Green, Hussar Blue, Polar White, Black
1970:	Savanna Beige, Middle Blue
1971:	Silver Mink, Tyrol Green
1972:	Middle Blue, Amber Yellow, Verona Green
1973:	Burgundy Red
1974:	Carolina Blue, Sunset Orange, Sienna Brown
1975:	Emerald Green, Coral White, Solar Red
1976:	Topaz Yellow, Opal Green
1977:	Antelope Brown, Dorado Brown, Marble White
1978:	Jade Green, Laguna Blue
1979:	Midnight Blue, Chamette Brown, Alabaster Yellow
1981:	Terracotta, Cirrus White, Cameo Beige
1982:	Admiral Blue, Maroon
1983:	Golden Yellow, Ivory, Cherry Red
1984:	Azure Blue
1984:	Finnish-built 99 two-door run-out models – mostly white, red, silver, silver blue, terracotta

Metallics:

1972:	Copper Coral
1973:	Sepia
1974:	Sterling Silver
1978:	Anthracite Grey, Cardinal Red
1980:	Carmine, Acacia Green, Aquamarine Blue
1981:	Indigo Blue, Pine Green, Silver, Walnut Brown
1982:	Moselle Green (Europe, six months only, no known UK 99s in this colour)
1983:	Slate Blue

Saab gearboxes of the era of the 99 could best be described as 'vintage' in their action and feel. Many had rattling chain drives (depending upon the tension) at idle, but most cars will have been worked on by now. Treated correctly, the normal gearbox will continue for at least 130,000 miles. However, common problems included bearing wear, often signalled by an increasing whine, and worn syncromesh. The primary chains can get noisy and some 'chatter' is normal. If they break, however, there is usually quite a big moment and bits of shattered gearbox housing and internals littering the road!

Early 99s also had a tendency to slip out of gear. On the early four-speed Turbos and on the five-speed Turbos, wear is even more obvious, as the box had to handle a great deal more power. Pinion-bearing wear on the four- and five-speed boxes was common, but rarely terminal, unless the gearbox was left to self-destruct.

The 900 gearbox has to be treated gently and drivers must take care not to rush changes. Any attempt to be rough with the gear stick would cause gear-selection problems. The stress of the turbo installation could also upset the gearbox as it digested the torque.

As with much of the engine work, attending to the gearbox means having the engine out, which is expensive.

This is particularly true of the automatic gearbox. With only three ratios, the engine and gearbox run faster and hotter than the manual; in the Turbo model, the gearbox is

---

Saab 900 Paint Shades

Original launch colours and new colours by year.

Solids:

1979:	Black, Cinnabar Red, Midnight Blue, Marble White, Dorado Brown, Chamotte Brown, Alabaster Yellow
1981:	Terracotta, Cameo Beige, Cirrus White
1982:	Maroon, Admiral Blue
1983:	Golden Yellow, Ivory, Cherry Red
1985:	Dolomite Sand
1984:	Azure Blue, Imola Red
1986:	Zircon Blue
1987:	Talladega Red, Florentine Yellow, Embassy Blue
1988:	Cherry Red
1989:	Ultramarine
1992:	Monte Carlo Yellow, Carrera White, Derby White

Metallics:

1979:	Cardinal Red, Aquamarine Blue, Acacia Green
1980:	Anthracite Grey, Carmine
1981:	Ruby Red, Pine Green
1982:	Moselle Green (a bright large-particled shade only available for approx six months, mainly in Europe), Red Gold (an early red-orange large-particle paint available in Europe; few in UK), Slate Blue
1983:	two-tone 900s, Slate Blue over Silver Metallic, Ruby Red over Silver (Europe/USA)
1984:	Amaranth Red, Platinum Blue
1985:	Rose Quartz
1986:	Odorado Grey (named after charcoal grey suits of Saab Italy importer Mr Odorado Pagani; a very popular colour that continues to this day), Malachite
1987:	Bronze, Silver (flat-particle), Cochineal Red
1988:	Rodonite Red
1989:	Ascot Grey
1990:	Iridium Blue
1991:	Le Mans Blue, Scarabe Green, Beryillium Green, Citrin Blue
1992:	Eucalyptus Green, Nocturne Blue
1993:	Ruby Red on 900 'Ruby'

---

really under pressure. Check the kick-down does not cut in at low speed, and check the belts and pulleys. Automatic gearbox rebuilds are not cheap and a reconditioned unit is often the better answer. Any high-mileage car that has not had the gearbox rebuild is going to need it sooner rather than later.

Clutch master-cylinder failures at moderate mileages was noted on some 99s and early 900s.

SUSPENSION AND TYRES

Check for rust in front wishbone mountings and rear arms.

In its lifetime, the 900 had many different suspension settings and a range of optional wheels. Between 1985 and 1993, there were apparently five different lengths of springs and twelve different spring rates. Notably, the Turbo 16S models, which pre-dated the similar 'Aero', had

These two cars are awaiting restoration. Their lack of corrosion underlines the quality of Saab steel.

the shortest and firmest spring/damper settings with lower ride height. The later 'Aero' was not as firmly sprung. The range of alloys also came in 15in and 16in sizes.

On the 99, the size of the wheel hub changed in 1970, so swapping wheels between early and late model 99s was not easy. Modifications were necessary to the hub carriers, for the larger hubs of the late cars.

Some owners fitted 205/50 section tyres to their 900s and lowered the ride height. This was the limit for the 900 and the tyres fouled the wheel arches and ruined the ride quality; 195/60 section tyres were a much better idea.

Abbott Racing has modified the engine and turbo of a number of 900s and can also advise with 900 suspension settings. The firm provided tuning and accessories in kit form and created its own niche as a bespoke Saab tuner. It was best known for its suspension /handling packages on the 900. The company now mainly caters for the newer Saabs.

Tyre choice on 99 and 900 Turbos can also be a serious consideration. Tyre manufacturers offer various options between wet-grip, dry-grip and longevity.

BRAKES

The Saab handbrake also works via the front wheels, so calipers need special attention. Partially seized calipers are a known problem. Similarly, 99s are known for squealing discs.

'Flat front' 900 – 1980s.

ELECTRICS

Not a known problem, but cars that have stood for a long time are bound to have wiring deterioration. The Saab fuse box under the front wing can get damp, causing connections to suffer. Wiring loom faults are not easy to diagnose. 900s can have circuit-board problems with connections in the fascia area.

STEERING

The heavy 99 steering can place a strain on rack mounting points. The later power-assisted set-up on the 900 is not troublesome. Thoroughly check out a right-hand drive 99 with power steering; there is no room under the 99's shorter snout for a PAS set-up without cutting into the wheel arches and wings, but power steering does apparently exist in right-hand drive cars. Many export model 99s with left-hand drive allowed power steering and air con to be fitted under the bonnet. Power steering was an option only on early 900 GLs and GLS models from 1979/80.

BODYWORK

The tank-like build quality of the Saab can give a false sense of security with regard to rust. The cars are made of steel that is thicker than normal and rust is not a serious problem, but it does happen.

The cars came with good undersealing and thick paint. For some reason, the two-door cars seem to resist body rot better than the three- and five-door cars. Indeed there was a period in 1977–79 when the hatchback 99 models seemed more vulnerable to rust than their predecessors.

Look out for rust in the doors, tailgate, rear wheel arches, bonnet and inner and outer front wings. The Finnish-built cars – notably the later 99s and 90s – were finished to very high standards and resist rot far better than earlier 1977–79 Swedish-built models. Again, there were differences in paint quality too, with some paints being thinner than others.

For a few short months, the early 900s were available in a light metallic green paint colour. This was later withdrawn, as it seemed to flake easily. Generally, the solid colours – notably the blues , greens and reds – lasted better. Elderly 900s will have fading paint by now, but hopefully it will not be flaking. Non-standard paint repairs can soon allow rust to take hold.

Both the 99 and 900 suffered a rust problem with their sunroof, which can be tricky to repair. The 99 could also rust in the large semi-circular scuttle plate behind the windscreen's lower rail, if any water had entered via the sealing strip over the years.

The earlier chrome-trimmed 99s and 900 suffered a rare problem in that the stainless chrome did not rot, but the clear plastic covering over the top of it, faded and coloured. This looked particularly bad on cars with chrome window trims, and sourcing the right replacement trim item can be difficult.

Of all the rust points, both the 99 and 900 need to be checked under the rear floor, where the fuel tank box and rear-seat lower cross-member butt up into the inner edge of the wheel arches. The sort of rot that can be found there will fail an MOT. Water and moisture can also accumulate in the fold of the pressing design and weaken the rear end. Older cars tend to sport two repair weld patches in each corner!

The 900s seem to be prone to a rust bubble on the front outer wings, where moisture seeping through from the inner wings can cause rot from the inside out. Bonnets on the 900 rust as well, notably on their lower edges from water trapped in the wing crowns, and repair is not easy. Doors rot in the corners and in the turned-under lower face.

Production Figures Totals:

99 model	588,643
90 model	25,378
900 model	908,817

Saab 99

Year	number of cars
1967	25
1968	4,190
1969	19,411
1970	29,755
1971	3,516
1972	45,001
1973	52,065
1974	62,637
1975	64,167
1976	72,819
1977	60,316
1978	45,851
1979	22,443
1980	17,108
1981	13,381
1982	20,006
1983	17,187
1984	7,145

Saab 90

Year	number of cars
1984	6,215
1985	11,385
1986	5,910
1987	1,868

Saab 900

Year	number of cars
1978	17,244
1979	52,748
1980	48,646
1981	53,011
1982	63,551
1983	78,825
1984	88,188
1985	86,707
1986	85,675
1987	83,163
1988	68,363
1989	54,035
1990	41,708
1991	34,833
1992	38,663
1993	33,577

*'Slant front'
900 – 1993.*

ACCIDENT REPAIRS

Look out for crash damage. Because of its inherent strength, the Saab, especially with the 5mph US-style impact bumpers, can take far more impact than other cars without showing obvious signs of deep-seated structural damage. A really heavy knock to a thinner-gauge car will show panel damage and chassis twisting, whereas any impact damage to a Saab will not be as obvious. The massive windscreen pillars and their legs can absorb enormous forces, and not show any damage, but when they are twisted or moved to the assymetric – say, from an offset frontal impact – they are extremely problematic to to re-jig and straighten.

It is imperative to check under and around any used Saab. Rear-impact damage can be spotted by ripples or repairs to the three-pronged rear chassis longerons, while the front wheel arches and box sections will show any serious crash repairs or damage. The front end is so strong that it can be twisted without any visible evidence; look out for uneven tyre wear.

Heavy repairs to a Saab are not easy. Watch out for uneven panel gaps and twisted panels, notably on Turbos, which will have been driven faster and crashed faster. One giveaway sign on both the 99 and the 900 is the area around the bonnet shut line at the scuttle and front doors. Any hint of the gaps being different on one side to the other, or of both being out of normal gap limits, is a sure sign that the car has a had a very heavy shunt. Similarly, if one front door fits with different gaps and hanging tolerances to the other, this may indicated a twisted body.

INTERIOR

Despite the major differences between the interiors of the 99 and the 900, the main items of concern remain the same:

the infamous headlining and the seat trims.

The outer skin of the one-piece fibre headlining tends to drop down and sag from the car's roof. Glueing, stapling and all sorts of other remedies have been tried. The only definitive solution is to remove the whole moulding and repair it outside the car.

The seats on the late 99s and early 900s featured diagonal ribbing and the seat covers have a tendency to pull apart from the ribs. Later cars had a different, harder-wearing trim design. The seat coverings on both models faded and wore through at tension points around the headrests. Leather trim on 900s lasted

well but are bound to be scuffed on high-mileage cars.

900s can suffer problems behind the dashboard with circuit boards and ancillary controls.

RARITIES

As time goes on, the classic car status of old Saabs is developing, especially early 99s, 99 Turbos and late 900 'Ruby' models.

The really rare classic members of the 99 family are the early-build chrome-bumpered cars with 94/96 trim fittings. The chrome-bumpered four-door saloon with the original dashboard was part of a short pro-

Despite their rust free status, wrecks like these are not worth restoring.
Note the inner wing structure.

duction run, and was soon superceded by the same body featuring the new dashboard design.

Other rarities include the early three-door Turbos, the limited-production five-door Turbos, and the early EMS models. Cars from the period 1977–79 tended to have more serious paint and rust problems than other 99s and are correspondingly rare.

Early-model 900s are thin on the ground too, notably the three-door EMS cars.

SAAB OWNERS CLUB

Any driver considering investment in a classic Saab would do well to join the Saab Owners Club. Rebuilding a wreck often leads to spiralling costs, but the club is an ideal way of getting access to information and spares, and at the same time making friends. Owners Club members can travel to an international meet every year somewhere in Europe or further afield, and special rallies also take place regularly.

10 Finale

According to the purists, the demise of the 900 saw the end of the real Saabs. Certainly, new Saabs are based on General Motors parts, so they are not Saabs in the sense that the 99 and the classic 900 were. However, Saab engineers are still hard at work in Sweden, creating that certain Saab spirit.

After Peugeot took over Citroën in the 1970s, the spirit of Citroën died and the marque entered the design doldrums, until a recent revival. At Saab, this has not been the case. The new 900 cleverly used 99 and classic 900 design iconography: the rising wedge body line, the peaked windscreen and turret shape, the lamp motifs and the curved tail. The 9-5 also recalls the styling of the original 99 and 900 Mk1. The new 900 became the 9-3, while the brilliant 9-5 has been a real success story and is recognized after Euro NCAP testing as the safest car in the world.

So, are the new cars really Saab designs mounted on GM chassis underpinnings? The fact is that Saab has always shared parts with other manufacturers yet remained true to its Saab ethos. A Triumph engine was used in the 99, and a Ford V4 in the 96. The Saab 9000 was a car developed by Saab, Lancia and Alfa Romeo, under a Fiat and Saab joint venture directed by the Wallenbergs and the Agnellis. The first Saab engine incorporated DKW ideas in its design. Furthermore, the first Saab aeroplanes were licence-built versions of German Heinkel, Dornier, and Junkers designs. Perhaps then, a Saab is a Saab, whoever builds it.

March 26, 1993 – the last 900 rolls off the Trollhätten line.

The 99 and the 900, notably the Turbos, were icons of a motoring age. Indeed, the Saab Turbo brand changed the face of automotive engineering and design, and in 2001 the sculptural 900 Turbo was exhibited in London as a piece of art. The 99 and the 900 brought safety, style and, eventually, turbocharged performance to the mass-market car buyer. Yet these highly unusual cars did not bankrupt the company. On the contrary, they ensured its survival and prosperity, and made the brand desirable. Surely General Motors would not have considered buying Saab without the Turbo legend.

The legacy of the 99 and the classic 900 is as stylistic antecedents of the new designs from Saab. The engineering ingredients are carried over, too. The spirits of Saab, the thinking of Ljungstrom, Sason, Mellde, Carlsson and Envall, all live in the feel of the GM-based Saabs.

In 1993, after a run of over a decade, the original 900 was withdrawn from production. 1992 had been a lean year for Saab, with near-static sales in some markets awaiting the new model and only the 9000 model existing above the 900 – and no

small Saab in sight either. At its death, over a fifteen-year period, the 900 had sold 908,810 cars – just short of the magic million mark. 48,888 of those were the late-conceived 900 convertible model.

Remember these cars' roots in their even older 99 model forebear and you have one of the longest-lasting designs in automotive history, alongside the Mini, the 2CV, and the VW Beetle. Given the esteem such names are held in, the quiet achievement of the 99 and 900 begins to shine through. If we remember the onward march of legislation that raised standards in safety and emissions, alongside factors such as road holding, fuel consumption and other dynamic ingredients, the fact that the 99 and the 900 remained ahead of the game for so long, surely speaks volumes for their depth of design integrity, and their designer's talents in the first place.

And in turning the solid, perhaps even staid 99 into the Turbo and then into the 900, there was no suggestion of sow's ear into silk purse – just proper design and development. The basic good ingredients simply got better, rather than being left to

The 'new' 900 – the subject of much debate by Saab purists, but still recognized as a Saab, nonetheless.

The 'new' 900 begat the 9–3. Both preserved essential Saab design details.

fester on the model range shelf or swept away, as so often done by other car makers.

So, whilst Saab wanted a totally new 900, they did not want to throw the baby out with the bath water. The Saab purists, of course, complained that the new 900 was not a true Saab, it was a General Motors car. Whatever, despite heated debate amongst the Saab buyers and club members, the new car soon made friends. Its Envall-inspired styling retained the curves and swoops of the original and had a rear rump of Sasonesque look. The floor pan was a strengthened unit from the Vauxhall/Opel Calibra coupe, and of course the aerodynamics and stability were superb. In dynamic terms the car was just off the target and these factors were attended to in a major revamp that created the subsequent 9-3 model in 1998.

The new 900 was launched as a five-door car and by late 1994 was available as a three-door coupe, then as a convertible.

The first cars had four-cylinder engines with balancer shafts, then a GM compact V6 engine of 170bhp arrived, giving the Americans a wider option. The first new 900s sold in Sweden for 200,000 Krona; in the UK the price was over £20,000. Sadly Saab's electronic auto clutch system, named 'sensonic', was too early for the 900's market and did not achieve great favour. Safety features rated highly, of course, notably a steel cross beam built into the back of the folding rear seat and a three-point belt mounting.

So, the Trollhattan Turbos, the Swedish flyers, grew into something different. Yet lessons and the legend of the 99 and the first 900 live on. The fact was that the original Saabs were unlike any other car. The 99 and 900 were the essence of Saab and the Turbo models represented milestones of automotive design and engineering history. As they say, cars are cars, but a Saab is a Saab....

Appendix I
Production Figures and Plant Output

Saab 99 –Production Figures by Factory, 1967–87

Factory of origin	99(2d)	99(4d)	99(3d)	99(5d)	90	Total
Trollhattan	205,456	71,892	60,863	8,901	–	347,112
Nystad	116,809	32,241	25,357	16,644	25,378	216,429
Mechelen (Malines)	16,677	814	–	–	–	24,821
Arlov	18,096	7,563	–	–	–	25,659
Total	35,703	119,840	86,220	25,545	25,378	614,021

Note: Saab Finnish factory at Uusikaupunki, Finland, produced over 200,000 Saab 99 models from 1971–84.

Saab 900 – Production Figures by Factory, 1978–93

Factory of origin	900 conv	900(2d)	900(3d)	900(4d)	900(5d)	Total
Trollhattan	–	–	219,940	123,518	85,255	28,713
Nystad	48,894	37,795	66,754	58,408	75,947	87,798
Arlov	–	–	57,259	83,770	31,502	72,531
Malmo	–	–	13,946	5,484	338	19,768
Total	48,894	37,795	357,899	271,180	193,042	908,810

OPPOSITE: A welder at work on the assembly line in the Saab factory.

Appendix II
Drawings and Details of the 99 and 900

Throughout the 99s life, numerous styling changes took place, mostly to grilles, lamps and trims. These drawings, courtesy of Gunnar A. Sjorgen, depict the changes to the 99 and 900 in accurate style.

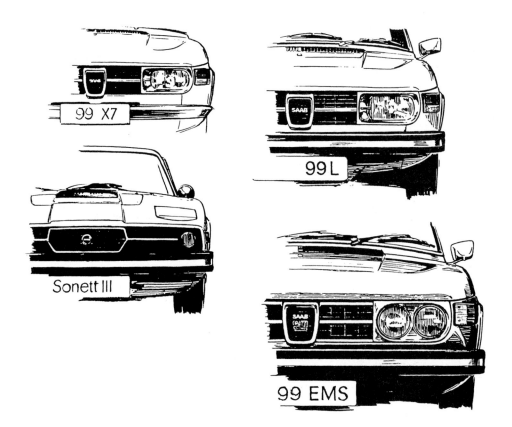

Grille and lamp designs for the early 99. The 'family look' grille also appeared on the Saab Sonnet Mk 3.

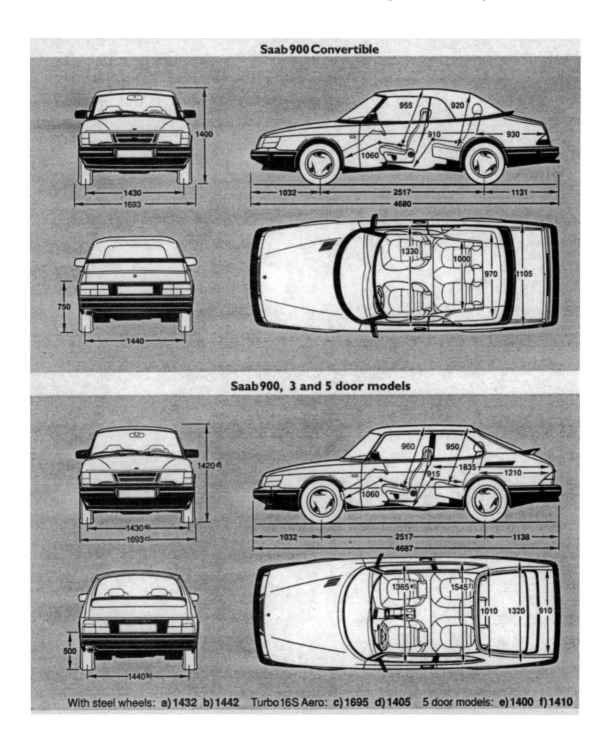

Saab 900 Convertible

Saab 900, 3 and 5 door models

With steel wheels: **a)**1432 **b)**1442 Turbo16S Aero: **c)**1695 **d)**1405 5 door models: **e)**1400 **f)**1410

Saab 900 dimensions. 1993 models.

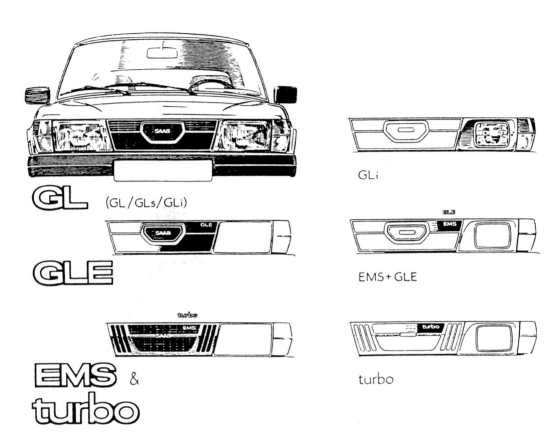

ABOVE: At its launch the 900 had a plethora of grilles!

OPPOSITE: These views of the 99 show the suspension dynamics and c.g. point.

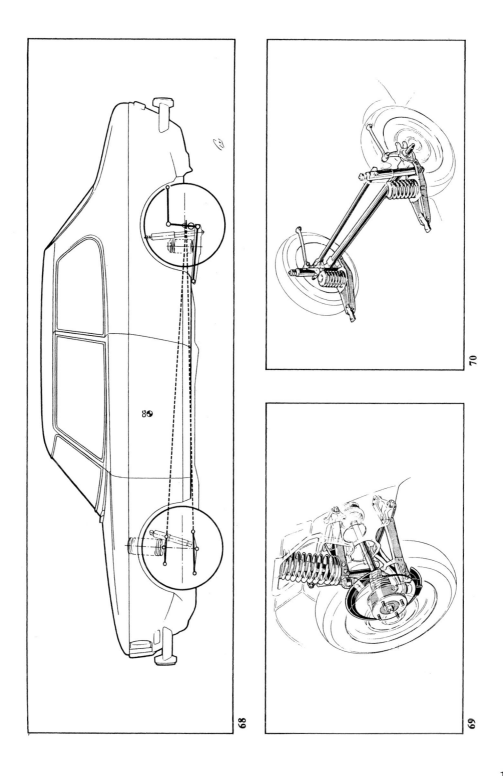

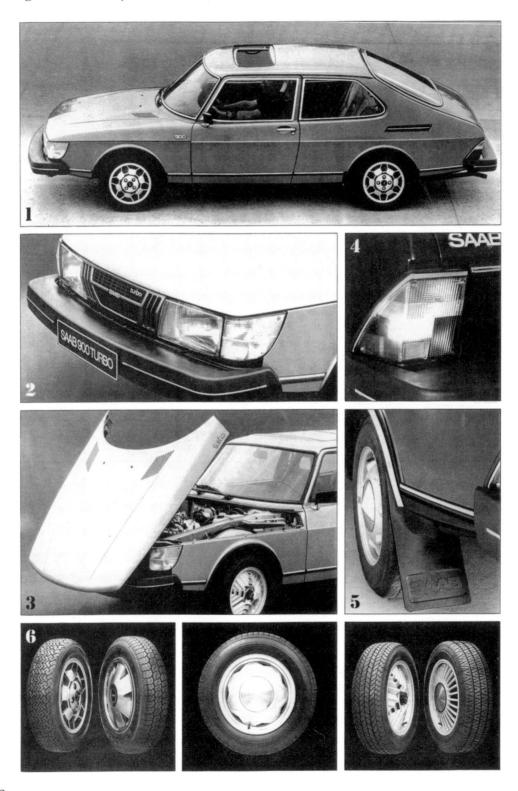

The interior with leather upholstery

The interior with Horizon velour upholstery

The interior with Parallel velour upholstery

ABOVE: *Late-model 900 interior trim styles circa 1992.*

OPPOSITE: *Details of the 900. Note the clever bonnet hingeing mechanism and various wheel trim options circa 1979.*

153

ABOVE: The Saab family in 1979. This is the cover of the Saab brochure of the day.

OPPOSITE: 99 Advert – USA 1969

Saab 99E
It's about time
a car was built
like this.

Appendix III
Summary Buyer's Guide

The following is a checklist of significant issues on the Saab 99, 900 and Turbo Models.

Turbo Unit
Check for functioning of turbo and waste gate.
Note turbo bearing or turbo seal failure signs: look for blue smoke from exhaust on revving.
Check for sticking waste gate and boost indication.
Note if water injection (99T) or intercooler (900) is fitted/functioning.
Ideally fit Viking Motors 99 Turbo intercooler conversion kit to 99T.
Check for after-market modifications.

Engine
Engine should start without throttle blip.
Injectors should fire easily.
Search for any gasket or cylinder head problems; check coolant and exhaust smoke for tell-tale signs. Early 99 engines had head problems.
Pressure spits, corrosion and warping to be checked for.
Note any excessive oil leaks on front crank seal or timing cover.
Ensure rocker cover seals not missing.
Camshaft wear is not common – this is a long-lasting item.
Sodium treated exhaust valves on Turbo cars fail and are difficult and very expensive to replace. Check for leaks and function on the water pump – this is difficult to replace.
Exhaust manifolds crack at cylinder 1 (99 Turbo).
Check timing and timing chain: if pinking is noted exercise caution due to possible piston damage. APC cars much better in this respect.
APC system on 16-valve cars must be functioning – it is expensive to repair.
Check two-point (990) and three-point (later 99 and all 900) engine mounts; loose mounts can affect gearbox/clutch alignment and distributor seating.

Gearbox
Early four-speed and then five-speed boxes will require work by now. Check for noise, chain gear rattle: if excessive, repair is expensive. This is a known problem on high-mileage 900s.
Turbo car gearboxes suffered bearing wear.
Check synchromesh on all cars – note if box deselects reverse.
Note that factory Turbos and after-market Turbo gearbox modifications had different ratios.
Gearbox whine is often evident.
Automatic boxes are prone to wear, especially on 900 Turbos. Major rebuild is an essential part of any 99 or 900 purchase. Check auto box function.

Suspension

Coil springs all round. Front wishbones. Check for mountings and arms. This is not a known problem area.

Brakes

Turbo cars can eat brakes; pads are hard to fit.
Seized calipers and squeaking brakes are a known 99 and early 900 problem.

Bodywork and Trim

Early 99 and late two-doors are most rust resistant.
Three- and five-doors of the late 1970s suffered greater corrosion and can be very tatty.
Paintwork repairs must be good quality.
The 900 is generally better lasting, but some 900s had paint work problems: fading solid colours and easily corroded metallics.
Ensure Saab factory-quality rust proofing and under sealing is evident.
The rust point under rear seat at outer corners by wheel arch is an MOT fail point.
99s rusted along lower wing to boot seam.
99 and 900s rust at door-fold underpoint.
Floor pan corrosion is rare.
Note inner and outer front wing corrosion, and bonnet rust, notably on 900s.
99 engine bay and longerons trap water, making this a corrosion site.
Sunroofs with blocked channels corrode and jam.
Seat trim wears through on all models, notably at the headrest to seat junction and squab edges. Headlining fails.

Cars to Buy

Values of the 99 model at time of writing extend from £250 for a wreck to approaching £5,000 for a rare and pristine early model basic 99. Good 99 Turbos in two- or three-door form fetch £3,000–£4000. Rare chrome bumper cars are appreciating, as are standard Turbos models. The likes of the five-door 99 GLE auto are not highly prized. Restoration costs can still outweigh the value.
Early 900 models with the first interior and seats are now rare, but early revised-model 900s can be bought for under £1,000 in road-legal and usable form. Late 1980s cars can be bought and driven daily from about £2,000. There are many specialist secondhand Saab garages and dealers who have a ready queue of 900 enthusiasts eager to snap up cars. Prices therefore remain firm, and rare or good cars can only appreciate. Late model 900 Turbos, notably the Ruby and the convertible models, are now an appreciating asset. Prices of up to £10,000 are, at the time of writing, still appropriate for such cars.

Further Reading

With a subject such as this, much information has been similarly used by others. Much that I have used has also been utilised by others, too. The following publications have offered the viewpoint of others as a reference point.

Dymock, Eric, *Saab: Half a Century of Achievement*, Dove Publishing, Sutton Veny/Haynes/Foulis, Sparkford, Somerset, 1997)

Elg, Per-Borje, *50 Years of Saabs; All the Cars 1947–97*, Motorhistorika Sallskapet I Sverge, Bondegatan 74, S-116 33 Stockholm

Sjogren, Gunnar A., *The Saab Way*, Gust. Osterbergs Tryckeri Ab, Nykoping, Sweden, 1984)

The Saab-Scania Story, Streiffert & Co Bokforlag Ab Stockholm, 1988

Transport Source Books, Ipswich, UK

Saab Owners Club of Great Britain driver magazine

Saab 99 and Turbo road test and articles

Motor and *Autocar* magazines

Technical spec information and history provided by Saab, Trollhättan

Saab 99 and 900 brochures 1969–89

Index